The Social Leadership Handbook

By Julian Stodd

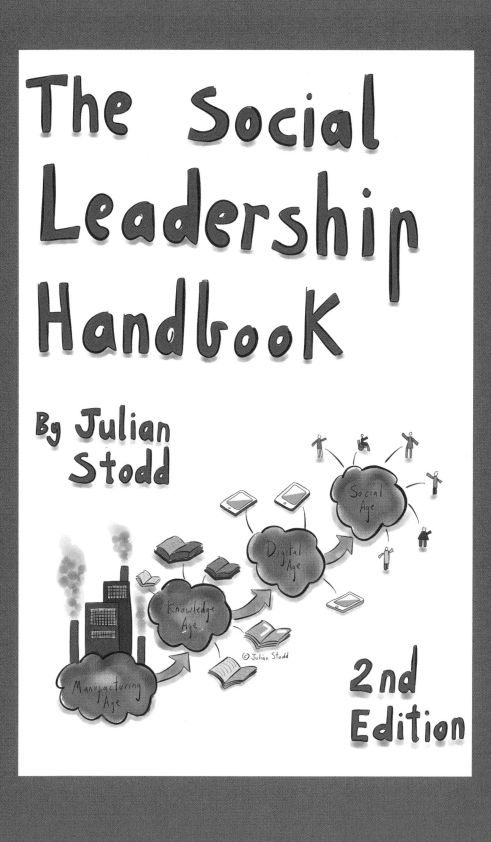

© Julian Stodd

2nd Edition

Printed in the United Kingdom
The Printing House
London | Chester

Design & Typesetting
SWATT Design Ltd.

2nd Edition printing, 2016
Reprinted, 2017

ISBN 978-0-9573199-7-4

Sea Salt Learning
www.julianstodd.wordpress.com
www.seasaltlearning.com

Table of Contents

The Social Leadership Handbook 2nd Edition — 5

Introduction to the second edition — 6
Prologue — 8
Introduction — 12

Part 1: The Social Age — 13

The Social what? — 14
The Social (and Socially Responsible) Business — 23
The Social Contract — 29
Social Collaborative Technology — 33
A note on 'agility' and what it has to do with Social Leadership — 36
Welcome to the Social Age — 37

Part 2: The NET Model of Social Leadership — 43

Overview — 44
The 1st Dimension of Social Leadership: Narrative in the NET Model — 46
The 2nd Dimension of Social Leadership: Engagement in the NET Model — 48
The 3rd Dimension of Social Leadership: Technology — 50
The nine skills of Social Leadership — 53
    1st Dimension: Narrative — 53
    2nd Dimension: Engagement — 66
    3rd Dimension: Technology — 81
Summary — 96
Developing Social Leadership: How do we train it? — 97

Part 3: Application 99

Six tenets of Social Leadership 100
Why Social Businesses, Leaders and Learners
need to understand amplification 102
Becoming a Social Leader: organisational strategies
for engaging and retaining talent 105
The Social Business: aligning Social Learning and
Leadership to the values-driven organisation 107
Social Leadership: communities and meaning 108
Why every business needs Social Leaders 110
The reputation of Social Leaders 111
How Social Leaders fight fires wisely 113
Social engagement and exclusion 114
The humble leader 116
The three levels of Narrative 118
    The three levels of Narrative: personal narrative 120
    The three levels of Narrative: co-created stories 123
    The three levels of Narrative: the organisational story 125
Story flow 128
Unheard wisdom 130
Global perspectives on Social Leadership: fairness 131
Ten things a Social Leader does 135
Aspects of Social Leadership: community 137
The new utility: a story about brand in the Social Age 139

Postscript 143

Postscript: Be The Change 144
About Julian 145

The Social
Leadership
Handbook

2nd Edition

Introduction to the Second Edition

Here we go again. It's a daunting thing, revisiting a book. In the old world, books represented collected, codified and fossilised knowledge. We wrote them, then we shared them. In the Social Age, they are just snapshots of what we thought at the time. What we think now resides in different spaces: on Twitter, in our stories, and for me, on the blog. Knowledge itself has changed, becoming more dynamic, adaptive, responsive and evolutionary. And, in response, books must change too. Retaining their core, but evolving their story.

At its heart, this is a guide to developing Social Leadership, for individuals and within organisations. Why? Because what we have is not enough. In the formal world, governed by hierarchies of power and control, positional authority was assured. But in the Social Age, formal and social spaces have converged, collided to form a new space. A grey space. A space not governed by old rules, possibly not governed by any rules that we have yet deduced.

Formal authority can never subvert social: it can drive conversations out of earshot, but it never kills them. Formal authority will only get us so far: for the rest of the journey, we need Social Leadership.

The heart of this book remains the model of Social Leadership: the nine components that form an image of and development pathway towards a more social and responsible way of leading.

Around it, my thinking continues to evolve: my language, as I rehearse and prototype it, becomes stronger, more coherent, more relevant I hope, especially because, as I write today, I've been fortunate enough to see this work embedded into practical application. In a number of organisations around the world, the principles of Social Leadership are being shared, adapted and refined.

Our world is imperfect.

Through the actions of organisations, governments and individuals, abusing and consolidating power, seeking profit over humanity, exploitation over empowerment, we exist in fractured cultures.

The actions of organisations fractured the Social Contract: the notions of '*career*', and even '*work*' or '*jobs*', are gone, replaced by portfolio lives lived out in multiple communities. We may inhabit organisations with our bodies, but our minds are our own.

If an organisation wishes to be dynamic, to survive, to thrive, it needs to engage the best people in the best ways. Social Leadership is part of that: creating a culture that is fairer, more equal, more kind, more effective and better performing.

I have spent the last two years working in organisations around the world, sharing this story: in banks and governments, military and third sector, manufacturing and oil, education and art. One thing is absolutely clear: we only have today to set the foundations for tomorrow. Ignoring, dismissing or belittling the challenges we face is a route to failure. What got us here won't get us through the rest of the journey.

Social Leadership is authentic, grounded and free to anyone to develop, adapt and share. The starting point is '*How can I help you to succeed?*', not '*How can I get you to do…?*'.

Humility sits at the heart of it: the humble leader, who is willing to learn, to share, to empower, to fight. Because sometimes we must fight: for equality, for fairness, for what is right, whatever the cost.

I deeply hope that you enjoy this book, that you find it both infuriating and challenging. I invite you to join the global community of thought that surrounds it, on the blog and in other online spaces. To learn is not to hear my story, it's to find your own. Take this, make it work, make it real, and help me learn what I need to learn when it comes time to rewrite it for the third edition.

Prologue

Let's start with the end in mind: Social Leadership encapsulates the mindset and skills required to be an effective leader in the Social Age. It recognises that power and authority are founded more on what you share and how you build your reputation than on simple positional authority. It's a model of leadership that is more fluid and relevant than those based on longevity, situation or hierarchy. Under a Social Model, sharing and narrating trump command and control. It's a collaborative venture with community at its heart.

The NET Model of Social Leadership is built around three Dimensions: *'Narrative'*, *'Engagement'* and *'Technology'*.

Each of these Dimensions is made up of three components, comprising the skills, concepts, models and attitudes of the Social Leader. The NET Model is both an idea and a call to arms.

This book is a guide for organisations looking to develop Social Leadership and for individuals looking to become Social Leaders.

The NET Model of Social Leadership is not intended to replace other models of leadership: it's complementary. It works in both formal and social spaces, recognising that, in the Social Age, we have to develop authority in both to be effective.

Being a Social Leader is about agility and fluidity of role: it's highly contextual and can complement other styles. At heart, it's anchored in the principles and ethics of value-led behaviour: it's about authenticity and support. You can't be a Social Leader all alone.

The '9 Components of Social Leadership' outlines a journey through the skills and mindset needed to be truly agile.

The first Dimension of Social Leadership is *Narrative*: this is about *curation*, *storytelling* and *sharing*. It's about you, yourself, inward looking, taking a stance and thinking about how you position yourself in your environment. It's about finding things out, finding the meaning in it and sharing it with relevant people, adding value as you do so. It's about being part of the conversation instead of part of the noise. Whilst Social Collaborative Technologies allow us to share easily, so much of what is shared, copied and reblogged is simply noise. To be effective, Social Leaders cut through the noise with relevance and clarity.

So Narrative is about:

CURATION – Finding things out and determining what's valid from what's just noise. It's about identifying networks and communities and seeing where the nodes and amplifiers sit. It's about quality and coherence, not volume and mass.

STORYTELLING – Do you know how to identify the Narrative that sits under the story? Can you find the meaning? Social Leaders need to be able to take their curated ideas and knowledge and forge coherent narratives, then flesh them out into stories that are relevant and timely to the audience. It's about understanding how stories are told and retold, so although the individual words change, the Narrative is constant.

SHARING – This is a core skill of the Social Age: curating content, finding the meaning and then sharing the stories effectively. This may be facilitated by collaborative technology, but it's not purely that. It's a mindset to share that counts: recognising that knowledge in itself is no longer enough. Great Social Leaders share to help others succeed.

In summary, Narrative is about **curating knowledge**, finding the **meaning** within it through 'sense-making' activities, **forming stories** and understanding how to **share** and **amplify** these. Narrative skills form the heart of personal effectiveness for Social Leaders.

Following on from *Narrative* is *Engagement*. Engagement is about:

COMMUNITY – Social Leaders operate in many communities, both formal and informal spaces where meaning is created. With Narrative, we looked at how to be an effective storyteller, with Engagement we are looking at the spaces in which those stories are told and how to use them to build your reputation and authority. This is about understanding why people engage in communities and how we can both form and sustain them effectively.

REPUTATION – As we move beyond purely hierarchical forms of power and authority, we enter the reputation economy. Reputation forms the engine of our effectiveness. If our reputation is weak, even if our stories are strong, we will struggle to get them heard or amplified. Reputation is forged in communities, founded on the quality of our stories and effectiveness of our sharing. Reputation can transfer from social to formal environments, but it's never conferred upon us by organisations. It's only ever earned.

AUTHORITY – Social Authority is born from reputation, based on the stories we curate. Authority in the Social Age is fluid, not fixed in bricks and mortar, and may be contextual. This component of Social Leadership is about recognising when and how that authority is exercised, about becoming magnetic.

In summary, Engagement is about understanding the **shape** and **structure** of informal and formal **communities**, understanding **how and why people come together** to work and learn. Reputation is the engine that powers our **effectiveness**: it's based on **actions**, not **hierarchy**, and authority is the outcome. We seek authority as leaders, but Social Authority is based on everything we've seen so far: curating knowledge, finding meaning, telling stories and understanding the ecosystem in which they exist.

Following *Engagement* comes *Technology*. This isn't about circuit boards and operating systems, it's about social collaboration, fairness and reach.

CO-CREATION is the process by which meaning is created within communities and the way in which culture changes over time. I use a seven-stage model of co-creation, often taking place within Scaffolded Social Learning environments. Co-creation is the sense-making process. Co-creation and the co-ownership of change are core concepts for the Social Age. Relevant to this are notions of the three levels of Narrative: personal, co-created in groups, and organisational.

SOCIAL CAPITAL is one's ability to survive and thrive in these spaces. Effective Social Leaders have high Social Capital and develop it in others. This generosity and humility reinforces reputation and authority. It's about keeping the field level and ensuring fairness and equality for all.

COLLABORATION is what it's all about: coming together and creating meaning, beyond that which we can do alone. Social Leaders collaborate widely: they engage in relationships without an expectation of immediate reciprocity. In time, all things balance out. The quality of how Social Leaders collaborate is what makes them effective and respected.

In summary, Technology is about *socially collaborative conversations*, about the *co-creation of meaning* in communities, about supporting *Engagement* and *development* in these communities and about *collaborating*, to achieve more than we ever can alone.

The NET Model of Social Leadership is a circle, because we keep moving around it. It's what keeps us agile!

The full NET Model can be represented in a circle: we start with 'curation' and end up at 'collaboration'. It's a circle because the journey never ends: once we have mastered the skills, we continue to refine them, and help others to achieve.

Introduction

This is a book about Social Leadership: a style of leadership that bridges the gap between the formal organisational space and semi-formal social ones. It's not an alternative to other leadership styles, it's complementary. And it's essential for any individual or organisation that wants to remain agile, to remain relevant in the Social Age.

In the first part of this Handbook, I'm going to explore the foundations for Social Leadership. This involves defining the Social Age, looking at the concept of *Social Collaborative Technology* and understanding how Social Leadership is based within communities on the reputation that we earn. We will explore how social styles subvert more formal leadership approaches and why Social Leadership is contextual, consensual and based on humility.

The second half of the Handbook is an exploration of the NET Model in detail: this is a structured curriculum based around three Dimensions and nine separate skills that Social Leaders need to develop to be truly effective.

Part 1: The Social Age

The Social what?

I use the term *'The Social Age'* to talk about the environment we inhabit today: it's a time when the very nature of work is evolving, changing to reflect a revised Social Contract, evolved technology and the rise of communities.

The Manufacturing Age, through Knowledge and Digital, into the Social Age: although a simplification, it represents the shift to a connected, liberally communicative world.

In the Manufacturing Age, we used to make stuff: banging together lumps of iron, burning coal, wrestling value from the very earth itself as we wrought iron and carved railways through the landscape, smelting and mining, until we outsourced it all and specialised production in a global network of trade and exchange, bringing us to the Knowledge Age. We convinced ourselves that this was OK: we no longer made stuff, but we had the knowledge, we did the clever bit ourselves and the knowledge was all that really mattered.

But then the internet evolved and Google was born, phones got smart and small, and our relationship with knowledge changed. In the Digital Age, we felt the bite of this technology: it fragmented from basement sized macro computers to pocket sized micro ones, and we started owning many devices that were both interconnected and semi disposable.

Many people assume that the Digital Age is the end point: that technology is the thing. But it's not. It's the underlying sociology that has changed. Finding stuff out is easy (and just see what happens when AI comes home to bite). Making sense of it is what counts. Welcome to the Social Age: facilitated by technology, but fundamentally about community.

Mechanisms of power and authority, which used to be gained through knowledge alone, are now based more in effectiveness, in being able to create value and meaning through the effective use of knowledge and resources in agile ways. Simply knowing stuff is not enough. Business models used to be based on hiding knowledge away, portioning it out behind paywalls and gateways, compartmentalising it, hiding it in books and charging for access. Free became the new way to add value and sharing became the differentiating behaviour. Why? Because the value of knowledge alone is being driven down to zero.

I recently gave a guest lecture at Dublin City University on *'Creating effective learning in the Social Age'*. It was a broad presentation, starting with how we communicate using stories, progressing to an exploration of a methodology for learning, journeying through mobile technology and Social Learning and ending up with some pragmatic steps for creating effective learning solutions.

The questions from the group were many and varied, reinforcing for me the value in taking time out to just think about how we communicate, how we learn. The thought that carried me through was that here we are, in the Social Age, even though many organisations haven't realised it yet.

As I heard stories of sectors trying to control and reject semi-formal spaces and resources, trying to restrict technology, trying to own the conversation, it made me realise just how far behind the times they are. Whilst, on the one hand, we see traditionally conservative industries such as finance or healthcare starting to experiment in pockets with innovative Social Learning and Leadership approaches, there are still many bastions of resistance, who fail to see that the walls are crumbling around them.

To deny change is not to dispel it.

Everything about how we work and play is changing. The fundamental structure of our society is evolving. How we communicate and, indeed, how we think, is in flux.

We are not at the dawn of the Social Age: we are already here and we're kicking down the walls!

Engaged

Dynamic

Tacit

Geolocated

Informal

Personal

Relevant

© Julian Stodd

The Social Age
of Learning

Supports
Agility

Contextual

Subverts
Hierarchy

Community

Devolved

Social

Adaptive

Extended

Co-Created

We are in the Social Age of learning. Formal hierarchies count for less
than our social communities and ability to create meaning.

The Social Age is about high levels of Engagement through informal, Social Collaborative Technology. It supports agility by allowing many and varied connections and the rapid iteration of ideas in communities that are *'sense making'*.

The notion of *sense making* is worth exploring further: it's about how communities iterate ideas, each member bringing their own perspective and interpretation and, collectively, finding the meaning. A large part of the power of the Social Age comes through the way that we operate within and alongside multiple communities, each of which may specialise or be generalist, but all contributing to this collective sense-making capacity. Our communities literally make us more effective than we can ever be in isolation.

'Sense making' is the activity we carry out in our communities: it's where we find the meaning.

Social Learning and Leadership approaches subvert formal hierarchy because they are powered by reputation, not formal status or longevity in role. Learning is extended and expanded as it moves beyond the purely classroom-based environment and into performance support and real-world application. In this context, learning is more directly owned by the individual and is highly portable: instead of existing in abstract, formal classrooms, it exists where you work.

Social Learning can be viewed as the semi-formal layers that surround the formal, the conversations that take place around it. It's the communities of learners who create meaning, rather than accepting what they are told without question. Social Learning is a mindset to rebel, to reach out and seek expertise and be unafraid to ask *'why?'*.

In this context, the role of the Social Leader is based on facilitation, mentoring and coaching rather than grounded in knowledge or formal hierarchy, both of which have diminished status. The skill is in creating communities of change, forming and working within these sense-making groups.

Technology facilitates the experience, it facilitates learning, but it doesn't guarantee it. The Social Age couldn't exist without it. It's the quality of stories we tell and the relevance to the individual that count, and today that relevance may be wider than simply the individual's current job.

As the fundamental bond of trust between employer and employee breaks down, as the notion of a *'job for life'* evaporates and we all become what Harold Jarche calls *'artisan workers'* to a greater or lesser extent, individuals who own our own skills and are responsible for our own development, the nature of the relationship with employers changes [http://www.jarche.com/2013/02/the-new-artisans-of-the-network-era/]. If I can't get what I want here, I'll go elsewhere. You can control the technology, but you can't control the conversation, and when push comes to shove, it's the conversation that counts. Technology is transient and adaptable. I can just bring my own device.

This is just one more example of how historical notions of control exerted by organisations over individuals are failing: technology used to be the preserve of the organisation, because (unless you were one of the geeks) only organisations had the purchasing power and skills to manage it. Now, with cloud-based services and every phone smarter than the Apollo Lander, mastering technology is not the issue: being productive with it is, and that's where communities count.

Stories let us join together in formal and progressively less formal groups, each supporting us in different ways. We have professional networks and social ones, each buoyed up by the same notion of Social Capital: our ability to survive and thrive online, our ability to form bonds, to be generous with our time and expertise, our ability to function as a valued member of the community.

Some of these communities are to do with our work, and may indeed be operated and *'owned'* by organisations, but the conversations are all our own. What many organisations fail to recognise is that if they close the space down or control it, the conversations that they don't like won't go away. They will just go elsewhere, where they are not part of them. We are so connected that our challenge isn't to find communities to join, it's to find time to service them all adequately.

The early attempts by organisations to moderate, own and control this have failed: you cannot control conversations by restricting technology, and you cannot drive engagement by telling people to talk. Instead of resisting the change, the organisation must become facilitating, enabling and empowering. By relinquishing control, we gain momentum.

One central observation of the Social Age is that we are able to maintain larger numbers of loose social ties, over wider geographies, whilst simultaneously building and maintaining an increased number of stronger and deeper ones. In other words, social technology lets us be more social, over wider distances. As our connections increase, we can specialise them and group them, so that we have different communities for different purposes: some technical, some subject-matter related, some purely social.

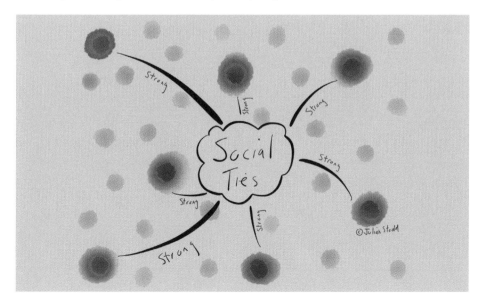

Anyone who looks for support just within the four walls of their organisation is missing a serious trick. In the Social Age, our networks can be broad, generalist or niche. I can turn to experts to help me with semantics, with technology questions, or with moral support. All of them are independent, all are able to travel with me wherever I go, connected to me through technology, but surprisingly resilient to background noise.

In the Social Age we constantly evolve. I can no longer afford to be static, I have to be an agile learner, able to reinvent myself in response to environmental inputs, in response to the feedback from my communities.

One of the questions from the university community was *'How do I narrate my learning?'*.

Like this... In iterative social spaces: tell your story, get it wrong the first time but be unafraid to try. Then listen to what people say and decide if you agree or not: this is the reality of the Social Age.

I'm not advocating that we entirely abandon formal learning (or formal leadership) – just the opposite: we embrace it, but surround it in progressively less formal layers where we can play with it. Where, in the language of our learning methodology, we can explore and reflect upon it internally. Where I decide how new knowledge stacks up against *'that which I know to be true'* and adapt accordingly, and external reflection, where I share my thinking with the community. It's learning squared, learning cubed, highly iterative, with knowledge as a foundation, but where meaning is co-created within the community.

This is the Social Age: technology has matured enough to facilitate our storytelling and enables us to seamlessly connect and form in meaningful communities. Organisations must adapt too: knowledge is no longer enough. Command and control is outdated, you can lock the doors, but the conversations aren't in the room any more, so it doesn't matter. They're here, in the coffee shop, and around the world.

This reality is the foundation for Social Leadership: the ecosystem is changing. Where meaning is created by communities that exist outside of the formal spaces of the office, we need leadership styles that can do the same. We need to be able to operate in both spaces, highly effectively.

The Social Leader, showing formal and informal space and the way that the Social Leader sits between the two.

What does this mean?

1. The Social Age is about creating meaning and doing it again, differently, tomorrow.

2. Formal and social spaces are colliding: Social Leaders need to be effective in both.

3. The value of knowledge alone is diminishing: it's no longer an effective source of power or sound basis for a business model.

4. Communities are sense-making entities that we rely on to support our performance.

5. Organisations that fail to adapt to the reality of the Social Age will become increasingly less relevant.

What should organisations be thinking about this?

1. Explore your organisation's stance towards knowledge: do you hoard it or share it?

2. Explore your relationship with your communities: do you engage or spectate?

3. Ensure your stance towards technology is fluid: the age of the dinosaur systems is over – are you constrained by your technology or liberated by it?

The Social (and Socially Responsible) Business

The Social Age requires Social Businesses: or, to be more precise, *Socially Responsible* ones.

Being a Social Business isn't about having a conscience or a great environmental policy, it's about being engaged with the realities of the Social Age. An age when the fundamental relationship between employer, employee and customer is changing. An age when change is constant and our ability to form alliances, build trust and remain agile is key. An age when technology isn't something that sits in a server room and needs air-conditioning, it's something that sits in your pocket and makes you more capable. It's an age when traditional hierarchies of power and authority are crumbling. It's here today and we all live in it. Even if we're not yet ready for it.

The Social Business is prepared to examine the status quo and adapt its processes, methodologies and culture. It engages in conversations with its leaders, its staff, its clients and even its competitors.

A truly Social Business will create spaces for experimentation, safe and permissive environments for development. Without this, we cannot change. Later, we will explore the nine core skills of Social Leadership, looking at how they are built over time, through rehearsal. They don't land fully formed.

There needs to be an understanding of risk, not an avoidance of it: avoiding risk can stagnate you. Quantifying it and using it makes you agile.

The Social Business benefits from Social Learning approaches and Social Leadership: it's values driven and engaged in all spaces.

Social Businesses recognise that they exist in formal spaces, which they own and control, but largely in semi-formal and informal spaces, which they don't. Their behaviour and conversations in these semi-formal spaces largely defines their future potential and certainly impacts on their magnetism. In the Social Age, brand is largely co-created by the community, not owned and dictated by the marketing department.

Broadcast models of brand, where we shaped it and imposed it on the market through volume, are eroded by social models, where brand is about community: interpreted and reinterpreted in the moment. Co-created and, to the surprise of many organisations, co-owned, at least in practical terms, if not legal ones.

Having effective conversations means you have to trust people, empower them to talk on your behalf, because, as far as the customer and community are concerned, the person talking to them on Twitter *is* the organisation. Hence, Social Leadership bridges the formal and social spaces and has to have authority in both.

This devolution of brand power and identity to individuals and out into the community is a key feature of the Social Age. Organisations still need process, but they don't need scripts: they need relationships with their teams that demonstrate trust and integrity, both things that build over time and form part of the new Social Contract.

In the Social Age, brand value is substantially created by community.

Synchronicity is important to Social Businesses: they respond in a timely manner, when times are good or bad, not just when they want to broadcast the news. A Social Business is proud to be right, but unafraid to say when it gets things wrong. It knows how to find out what the *'buzz'* is, because it has its ear to the ground, and it builds a reputation for responding honestly and meaningfully. A *'company philosophy'* has no meaning: responding to my tweet does. Listening to my concerns and responding is more powerful than just acknowledging that I'm annoyed. Social Businesses respond in a timely manner, whatever the story.

Technology forms the backbone of Social Businesses, crossing both formal and informal types, but above all, it's used to facilitate experience, it's used for communication (both internal and external, to enable individuals to engage). It's used for collaboration (for formal and informal communities). It's used for facilitation – to deliver scintillating customer journeys, learning journeys, development journeys and employment journeys. It's used to support products and services with active engagement in communities, and to respond to challenges. It's used to support excellence, and there is a mindset for technology, not just policies.

Social Leaders are not just grown from within, they are attracted from outside. The Social Business is magnetic to talent: not only does it grow its own Social Leaders and socially engaged teams, but it's also viewed as a place to be. Its reputation precedes it, in the labour marketplace as well as the consumer one. Being magnetic to talent isn't about being a Silicon Valley giant: it is about trust and integrity, about equality, about flexibility, support and freedom of expression. It's about living values, not capturing them in a handbook.

Agility in relationships is important, too: internally, recognising that careers include raising families and taking holidays, but also externally in agile relationships with suppliers, partners and associates. We recognise that, in Social Businesses, not everyone vital to our success is within these four walls and that not everyone wants to be here forever: it's about sailing on the high seas but knowing who else is around you, and maintaining good relationships with as many as possible. In the Social Age, people come and go, but networks and relationships persist: your ability (and the ability of the organisation to maintain these relationships) is a key differentiator.

And most of all, Social Businesses can learn (within those experimental spaces they've created): they make mistakes and learn from them, they experiment and learn from it, they listen to their teams, their communities and their customers, and they respond. They are bold and they are agile: able to create meaning today and to do it again tomorrow.

The social ecosystem is complex: individuals operating in open communities, engaged with various businesses in varied ways, supported by social technology and delivering innovative goods and services to a client base that ultimately owns the brand. Building trust with these communities, especially for big businesses like banks that are bruised, is tough.

Organisations need to develop social mindsets: they have to understand the ecosystem and be able to operate at the speed and with the agility required to thrive. They have to cultivate meaningful relationships, social contracts with their employees. Because if they don't, they won't be here tomorrow to feel the benefits.

The Social Age sees a changing nature of work: the office is dead, replaced by agile and mobile working methods, global collaboration and a changing relationship with knowledge. Whilst organisations used to operate in silos, constrained within the granite walls, today the walls are in our heads. The question of the responsibilities of a Social Business is a wide one. Where there is no long-term continuity of employment, where our development is in our own hands (because businesses focus on reactive and immediate responses to the pressure of change), we need a stronger Social Contract in place.

Legal and ethical imperatives may vary: but an organisation's responsibility is to curate a strong reputation through thought, act and deed, and the contract with employees forms part of this. This is beyond simply having a sustainability policy and exploring carbon offset: it's fundamentally about how organisations treat employees and how they reap the benefits of operating fairly (as opposed to simply complying with legislation).

We see this clearly around gender equality: it's possible to comply with the law whilst still remaining an unequal employer. We shouldn't need to wait for the legislation to catch up to realise that simple things could be made better. Why can't maternity leave be split between both parents? If we fail to recognise that either mother or father could be the primary caregiver at home, we are complying with the law, but breaching a social responsibility. A responsibility to be fair.

If we simply react to pressure to change, we are blowing in the wind: the Socially Responsible Business leads the change, and it does so because it's the right thing to do. This is a business to be proud of, a business that will attract and retain the best talent.

The culture of an organisation is co-created by both individuals and the organisation itself: framed by the company, but lived by the people. The small decisions impact upon it as much as the larger strategic drives. For example, where the company pays tax is a strategic decision, but also one that impacts on culture. And, indeed, impacts on brand value, because the value of the brand, as we have seen, is owned largely by the social community that surrounds it. These are disproportionately significant issues, amplified stories that spread around the world.

Learning informs brand value: an organisation that supports learning, that values it, will be stronger than one that doesn't. Agility is gained through the ability to create meaning and respond to change, a capability born from mindset as much as from technology or strategy.

The Social Business needs to be aware of all these issues: it needs a Socially Responsible contract with employees, it needs a socially aligned strategy and it needs to listen as much as to talk. But none of this should be seen as fluffy or soft: in the Social Age, I believe that only those businesses that face up to these challenges have a future. The reputation economy is here: how we are perceived matters.

It's good to see many businesses taking up this challenge, but they need support at every level and we all have our part to play. Responsibility is a mindset, not a policy.

We need a holistic pattern of adaptation: not simply one system, one process, or one person, but a different mindset, based upon doing what's fair, what's right, what needs to be done.

What does this mean?

1. Social Businesses recognise that their responsibilities go beyond complying with what's legal: they need to do what's right.

2. They recognise that, even though the nature of work is changing, they have a responsibility to develop and support Social Leaders and workers.

3. Reputation counts more than anything.

4. Brand is owned by the community, not the marketing team. Actively curate it.

What should organisations be thinking about this?

1. Are their processes, mindsets and methodologies for business anchored in compliance or responsibility?

2. Is the culture fit for purpose?

3. Do they understand the function of the office: is it where meaning is created, or is it an outdated monument to older forms of power and authority, status and reputation, now subverted by more agile modes. And, if that's the case, do they have a plan to deal with it?

The Social Contract

Are you still going to be in that job next year? In five years? Twenty? Chances are that none of us have a job for life, or that we expect to have one. Whatever counts as a career these days is largely a fiction, replaced by a curated series of jobs, some good, some bad, some convenient, others desperately risky but fun. Careers these days are fragmented. They evolve, fracture, make unexpected turns and leaps and take us in surprising directions, only some of which feels under our control.

In older ages, the organisations we worked for owned our careers: from your first graduate position right up to your first promotion, your team leader role, management and, eventually, a corner office, parking space and seat on the board. Then, one day, they would give you a carriage clock and send you on your way, into retirement, your useful and productive days behind you. Nothing to show for it except a battered leather briefcase and a vague sense of loss.

But no more: today, you'll be made redundant twice before you're thirty-five and the chances of getting a parking space are slim. A bike scheme, maybe. Instead of a large office and membership of the executive lounge, you're more likely to oversee a range of *'change'* projects and then be part of a transition team as your company merges. Then you'll spend six months in consultation before they say *'thanks – and goodbye'*, leaving you with enough money for a month in India before you start again.

You'll join a start-up technology company, go bust, be bought out, grow a beard, get a tattoo, lose the beard (apologies for the gender bias – but sadly, that reality remains all too real: if you are female, you'll earn less than me for the same job and be expected to come back from maternity leave – yes, as the primary caregiver – and take a lower position. Sorry.). And retirement? In the reputation economy, that's a far more fluid affair. You will be valued in alumni and expert groups for years to come.

But the Social Age is not about abandoning the values and principles that govern good employment: it's about expanding and enhancing them. The Social Age requires a Social Contract between employer and employee, based upon fairness, values, integrity and support, but recognising that the very nature of employment has changed.

Organisations used to provide the four walls of an office and a telephone, computer and chair: but what use are these in the Social Age? Infrastructure used to be hard, used to be valuable, but today, I just want good coffee, free WiFi and clean public toilets. I can get all of that without working for anyone. The office is wherever my iPad sits and the beige walls constrain me far more than they enable me: the Social Age is about creating meaning, about effectiveness and transformation, riding the waves of change, not paddling along behind them. Just as the requirements of work are changing, so too are the things we need to look for in the Social Contract.

Everyday pressures drive organisations to look for the lowest common denominator, but that has to be countered by the need to be magnetic to talent in a global marketplace. Social Leaders will be developed from within and attracted from outside, but only if there's a fair Social Contract in place: we have to recognise that magnetism is important and people have choices.

It's not enough to be cost-effective and streamlined if you can't attract or retain the very best talent, because that talent is what will make you agile, what will make the organisation dynamic. It's what gives you creativity, and creativity is the magic that will keep your organisation in play five years from now. Innovation around products, services, structure, cost models and technology: innovation is essential to any healthy organisation, but as the Social Contract fails, it's harder to find. You cannot simply pray for innovation and creativity: you have to create the conditions for it to occur.

A truly social organisation must pay heed to this and go beyond the traditional metrics and bounds of employment: it must do what's right, not what's legislated for. A Social Business needs to recognise the evolved nature of the marketplace and understand the drivers and pressures on those that inhabit it.

A Social Business needs to support the development of skills and behaviours that will allow us as individuals to thrive in this job, then help us to get the next one. If we recognise that there is no longer a job for life, the very least we can do is ensure that we attract the best talent, develop it whilst we are aligned, and leave on good terms. In a portfolio labour market, chances are that we will work together again down the line anyway.

Indeed, I recently had a conversation with someone on the benefits of recruiting on the strength of the exit plan: discover where the candidate wants to be in five years time, what job they will be applying for elsewhere, and work to help them get there. Sure, they'll leave, but imagine the fun you'll have along the way.

When it comes to things like maternity and paternity leave, don't lag behind, don't take the most defensive position possible. Be bold, be brave and do what's right, offering equal terms to both parents. We can be dragged kicking and screaming into the Social Age, or we can be pioneers, brave adventures, explorers driven by the notions of what is right, fair and equal. Better to be brave than insipid. If you want authentic leadership, you have to earn it. Words are just words until backed by action.

The Social Contract should recognise that the walls of an organisation are highly permeable: people belong to communities that transcend geography and sector. Our brand, the reputation of the business, resides largely in those spaces. Have a bad reputation and you can't be magnetic to talent, and if you're not magnetic to talent, you're not in a good place at all.

Imagine the conversations that took place out of earshot in the organisation where a leader asked someone in his team how they could edit a Glass Doors review. Glass Doors is a website for rating employers: social scoring of formal systems, devolved power and authority, claimed by the community and used to subvert the formal authority of the organisation. Sure, you can influence your Glass Doors score: you do it by being better, by doing better.

The Social Age presents challenges and opportunities to both employer and employee: as the fundamental mechanics of the workplace evolve, driven by both technology and social pressures, we need to adapt, but not to retreat to the most conservative place and lowest common denominator. We need to be bold, to implement a new Social Contract that recognises these evolved realities and leaves an organisation able to face this challenge with pride.

The old Social Contract is gone: it's not coming back. The world we inhabit is one created through the actions and faults of the formal hierarchy: they broke the trust and it's down to them to earn it back again.

In the Social Age, engagement will be earned, not bought, it will be dependent upon action, not promises. The mechanisms of Social cannot be easily cheated, and perish the thought that you try to do so and get caught out. The amplification of good stories is as nothing compared to how fast the bad ones move.

Throwing your weight around used to count, when mass meant something. Today, the weight lies not in mass, but in story, in authenticity, in fairness. Being good counts.

So tear up the old and be part of the new: Social Leaders will pioneer a new Social Contract within their organisation. Explorers of a fairer age. True to themselves, true to their communities. The communities that will help them, in turn, to succeed.

What does this mean?

1. As the Social Contract evolves, sticking with older models of recruitment and development will leave you wallowing in the shallows.

2. A fair Social Contract will increasingly make you magnetic to talent: talent which is hard to find and harder to keep, but which is essential for agility.

3. To build reputation, we have to do what's right, not just what's legislated for.

4. We may have to pioneer a way, not just copy the others. Be guided by our communities.

What should organisations be thinking about this?

1. Is your Social Contract balanced?

2. Are you developing enough long-term skills within a population, or do you fear that this will just enable people to leave for the next job?

3. Are you striving to survive, or striving to be fair?

Social Collaborative Technology

The correlation between technology and Social Leadership is clear: without the technology, you can't be a Social Leader. You can be a sociable one, but that's a different thing altogether. Social Leadership is grounded within and alongside our communities, those communities that consist of wide and loose social ties combined with a number of strong and deep ones, independent of geography and, increasingly, language.

Social Collaborative Technology is that which connects and facilitates us: this is the most important thing to understand. The technology itself is irrelevant: it's the facilitation that counts.

The clue is in the title – it's effortlessly social. It's everywhere: on our networks, in our pockets, plugged into our ears and our TVs. We can't escape the proliferation of Social Collaborative Technology, wherever we try to hide. It draws us into communities around our favourite reality TV show, it permeates our choices of which books to buy and what device to read or listen to them on, it lets us run projects worldwide and, if we are very lucky, it helps us to make sense of the world around us.

The Social Age is founded upon social technology for collaboration and we are just at the start of recognising the potential that it will bring. For Social Leaders, who rely on the amplification and sense-making functions of these communities, it's the technology that connects them, that enables them to collaborate.

When I wrote about Mobile Learning, I called the book '*Mindset for Mobile Learning*', because it's not about the technology per se, it's about what we do with it, how we craft more effective and dynamic learning experiences through that technology. Which chipset it contains may facilitate that capability, but it's not the direct cause. It's the same with social collaboration, as many organisations know to their cost: you can invest all you like in systems that have '*social*' in the title, but if they're not truly collaborative technologies, they won't build a community and they won't help you to create meaning.

Organisations have to move beyond ownership and into engagement. Don't seek to own the boxes, devices and cables, seek to engage in the conversations.

Truly Social Collaborative Technology makes it effortless for us to engage, to curate and to share. Like Facebook. It's virtually synchronous, which makes our encounters more conversational, more about storytelling than about publication. True social technology is agile and links easily: it doesn't tie you in with licence agreements, platform-specific functionality and endless login and registration pages. Truly social technology is about experience, not IT skills.

On my iPad today I have a hundred and forty apps. I use thirteen. What are the odds that the organisation backed one of those thirteen? We live in a time of evolutionary technology, technology that adapts, connects and at times is disposable.

The dinosaurs are dead: I believe that the time of those large, legacy systems that cost a fortune to install and never really did what you expected are gone. The future is about smaller, more interconnected technology that fits the Social Model: it talks to other systems, generates meaningful analytics and lets you act upon them easily. It adapts to context and location.

We were out walking yesterday, a group of friends from university, and the discussion turned to books: but instead of which books we were reading, we were talking about the ways we consume the content. Kindles, Kobos and iPads, even audiobooks. There was a constant theme: none of us had the answer. We are all experimenting, finding our way. There is no one system that is going to deliver all the functionality and features that you need to support Social Learning and Social Leadership. There may well be one mindset, though: a mindset for curation, sharing and collaboration. A deep-rooted curiosity. Mindsets persist whilst technology goes through an endless cycle of development and updates.

Get your mindset right and the rest will fall into place: it's all about collaboration and finding technology that facilitates it. It's about recognising that the people who find it may not be your IT department. The future organisation will recognise that its challenge is not one of control, of preventing people experimenting and collaborating, but rather one of learning from that interaction. And helping people to share the story of what worked.

What does this mean?

1. Social Collaborative Technology is at the heart of the Social Age.

2. It powers collaboration and is effortlessly social.

3. Organisations have limited capability to manage the 'effortless' part of this and, indeed, often cripple the attempt.

4. We need a mindset for technology that involves curiosity, experimentation and agility.

What should organisations be thinking about this?

1. Don't try to procure a solution to social collaboration. Look for where the conversations are happening and try to engage – on the community's terms.

2. Owning technology, controlling behaviours, is not a win. Collaboration and co-creation is the win. Aim for that.

3. Listen to wisdom wherever it emerges: count yourself lucky that you can hear it.

'Agility' and Social Leadership

Social Leaders make an organisation agile. What is agility?

It's about **QUESTIONING** everything. Just because you did it that way yesterday doesn't mean you should do it that way tomorrow. In the Social Age, change is constant. Doing what you always did won't work anymore. Question everything. It's a good habit for agility.

LEARNING is constant if you're agile. If you're not learning, you're stagnant, lethargic, stuck. Agile learners reach into their networks and communities to create meaning. They use technology to access knowledge and refine it, filter it, share it and tease out the relevance.

REFINING is the process of filtering out the meaningless and contextualising the rest. Agile learners and Social Leaders do this constantly, curating a reputation for quality.

DOING is better than thinking too hard. Agility is about getting stuck in, but constantly refining. It's an action research mindset, about making mistakes and learning.

MISTAKES are inevitable: organisations that want to be agile need to create permissive environments for us to trip up in as we learn.

EDITING is how we refine our actions, how we make the small changes that make us agile.

NARRATING is core to agility: do it, then reflect on it, then share how you did it.

SHARING everything.

In the Social Age, only the agile will thrive.

Welcome to the Social Age

So here we are: the dawn of the Social Age.

Our world has changed: many of the fundamentals that served us so well for so long are evolving into new, uncertain and impermanent structures. Technology is one of the most visible manifestations of this change, but the change is much more widespread than that: the underlying sociology and, possibly, psychology has changed too. The notion of 'a career' is just a fiction, now owned by individuals rather than the organisations they temporarily work for, Social Authority subverts formal control, and authenticity counts for more than your marketing budget. The 'broadcast' model of communication has been trumped by the co-creation of stories that are themselves co-owned. Brand is controlled by the community. And we see new forms of power evolving, facilitated by technology, founded upon reputation, and effective in socially moderated spaces. Welcome to the Social Age. And this is just the start.

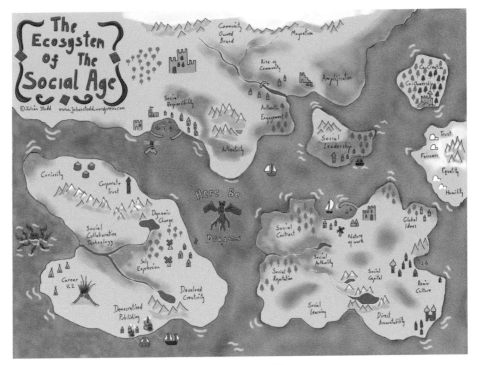

A map of the Social Age

The point of this chapter is to provide an overview – a snapshot of the landscape as we see it around us – and to start to think about how we can adapt our personal and organisational strategies and working practices to enable us to thrive. What got us here will not get us through the rest of the journey: organisations that fail to adapt will lose relevance and momentum. This is the reality of the Social Age: agility and a capability for dynamic change are essential.

Why the '*Social*' Age? Well, because it feels to me to be transcendent: we saw the Age of Industry, where Victorian powerhouses concentrated wealth around manufacturing and invention. We saw the Age of Knowledge, where knowledge was concentrated in books, libraries, universities and formal entities of authority. But that is itself being overtaken by the Age of Dissemination, where '*facts*' are available on demand and we rely on the '*sense-making*' capability of our communities to do something with them.

We can talk about the '*Digital Age*', but for me that represents a mindset of technology, which is only one part of the change. Digital is a technological pressure, but we inhabit the social.

Why a map? Maps are abstractions of reality: cartographers survey the landscape, explore new places and capture it all on a chart. But it's never complete: things change, new spaces are discovered, events change the environment, sometimes deliberately, sometimes through disaster or erosion. It's a constant process of change. The map captures current understanding, and we can use it to navigate, but it's not a solution: it's a picture of the ecosystem we inhabit and the areas we will have to pass through to hope to find our way. Let's explore this new world in some detail.

Social Leadership sits near the middle: the rise of non-hierarchical, socially moderated authority. It's one of the most significant changes in the ecosystems we inhabit, for a number of reasons. Firstly, formal and hierarchical authority does not transfer into social spaces, and it's in the social spaces where much of the '*sense making*' is done and our reputations are built. So lacking Social Leadership capability disadvantages us as individual leaders and as organisations. And it's a double hit: first, we lack authority, and second, we lack the ability to build that authority and make sense of the new world. It's a high priority for organisations to address this.

Similarly, Social Learning is about the evolution of learning away from formally defined, time-bound and organisationally driven experiences, and towards co-created, longer-term and more performance-outcome-based approaches. Or rather, that's what we should be aiming for: the days of tedious eLearning and lectures are numbered. To be truly dynamic, an organisation needs to be a learning organisation, with a mindset for learning embedded in everything it does.

To which point, we need Socially Collaborative Technology, one of the more visible battlefronts of this revolution. The old systems of power and control are being replaced and eroded by more agile, lightweight and intuitive ones, often tying into (social) tacit and tribal knowledge. This is at direct odds with the solutions that some vendors are pushing, which are still based on rapid authoring and quantitative analysis of interaction, neither of which is necessarily good.

Social technology has facilitated enhanced communication: barriers of time and geography are removed, enabling us to develop and maintain wider communities of loose social ties (as well as deeper, stronger ties with certain people over wider geographies). This drives community formation and function: stronger, wider, deeper. We can view technology as a driving and facilitating force, but it's matched by evolved social skills, particularly driven by social networking. We have learnt through Facebook and its ilk to live in online communities, developing curatorial and publishing skills to thrive in these spaces.

The excuses I hear most often from organisations as to why Social Learning or Leadership isn't for them are always along the lines of *'our community don't really get technology'* or *'they never engage'*. There's a reason for that: it's because more often than not the technology on offer is redundant, tightly controlled and non-permissive for experimentation, and the reason people don't engage is because it's not effortless or it doesn't make them more effective. Once organisations realise that they don't need to own everything and have a central city office to be magnetic to talent, to have status, they can start to be more agile, more responsive, more effective.

One of the most fascinating changes technology has brought us is an evolved approach to publishing, with every device of consumption being a device of production. As Clay Shirky taught us, publishing is democratised through multitudinous software solutions. From WordPress to Twitter and Facebook, Yammer and LinkedIn (and a million others), we can share easily. We can produce videos, animation, music, photos, any creative and collaborative venture with ease.

So collaborative technology and democratisation of publishing power change. Publishing directly supports curation and reputation, two of the components of the NET Model.

Some radical changes in work itself form a backdrop: career has been replaced by a series of jobs, some of which you may be paid for. Ownership of our own long-term development now largely sits with us and our immediate community, not with our employer and their career path. The Social Contract, which exchanged our time for money and security, has been torn up. Both these changes lead to a different form of engagement between organisations and individuals: unless we want a relationship that is based on convenience and desperation, we have to earn a relationship that is based on trust and mutual value. One which requires effort on both sides.

You'll see that my recent work on the Dynamic Change Framework has left its mark here, as I've decided to include it on the map: organisations that cannot surf the waves of change are doomed to ever-decreasing relevance and ever-increasing lethargy. There is no shortcut to success: just the need to adopt a constant pattern of curiosity and adaptation. Organisations need to wire change into their DNA, so that they do it effortlessly, not whilst gasping for air.

In the Social Age, we live in a remix and co-creative culture, in which the only certainty upon publication is that it's now out of date: more dynamic ways of working are required, more co-creative storytelling and greater co-ownership of the responsibility and results. Working out loud and sharing our learning as we go.

Authenticity erodes marketing and curiosity subverts false stories. Only through authentic engagement and open storytelling can we thrive. On which note, spot the new island in the East: I've grouped Fairness, Equality, Humility and Trust together over there, seeing them as core traits of the adapted organisation and effective leader.

Culture is important in any map of change in the Social Age: I've been exploring how cultures form and respond to change, working on a model of slow degradation followed by fracture. It's about alignment of core values and outward behaviours: what does it cost you to be in a culture?

Finally, we come to our evolved relationship with knowledge: as we recognise the true impact of the reputation economy and the Social Age, what you know is less important than what you can do with it, your ability to create meaning.

To navigate the Social Age, we need certain skills: Social Leadership, collaboration, curation, storytelling, humility, sharing. It's a long list, but success comes through proper planning. And none of it is rocket science: it's about understanding the environment and ensuring we remain agile as we navigate it.

Taken together, the changes we see around us in the landscape of the Social Age are broad. Some of what we hold to be true still exists, but much has changed. And bear this in mind: failure is often sudden. The difference between 'poor' and 'good' is wide, but the difference between 'good' and 'excellent' is vast. And if you aren't striving for excellence, you're at risk.

I talk about the 'ecosystem' of the Social Age, because that's how I see it: the environment that we live in. And the thing we know for sure is that as the ecosystem changes, we have to adapt if we want to stay fit. Those who fail to adapt become extinct. And thinking about adapting is less useful than actually changing.

My own work is to explore, document and share my understanding of this new world, this Social Age. But it's a co-created effort: if you don't like my map, draw your own. And if we both share them, listen to each other with humility and respect, maybe we will draw a new one together.

The Social Age is upon us: the choice is simple – adapt or fail. And ask yourself the question: is your organisation fit yet?

What does this mean?

1. We are in a time of constant change: we cannot adapt to the new space as though it were static. We have to continuously evolve.

2. Old skills may no longer be relevant: we need skills for the Social Age.

3. As our relationship with knowledge evolves, as the ability to create meaning defines the Social Age, the ground is ripe for Social Leadership.

What should organisations be thinking about this?

1. They need to understand the ecosystem, to read the map.

2. Formal authority is past its sell-by date: develop Social Leadership capability. Fast.

3. Understand who is responsible for this change. Will you be able to co-create and co-own it?

Part 2: The NET Model of Social Leadership

Overview

In the first part of this book we explored the foundations of the Social Age. Now it's time to look at the NET Model of Social Leadership in detail. It's called the NET Model after the initials of its three Dimensions (some creative thinking applied here...): *'Narrative'*, *'Engagement'* and *'Technology'*.

'Narrative' is about *curation* (knowledge management and sense making), *storytelling* (communication skills and storytelling culture) and *sharing* (adding value and building reputation).

In *'Engagement'* we break into the importance of building *community* (both formal and social), *reputation* (exploring how we use a magnetic model to build it and how it subverts hierarchy in the Social Age) and *authority* (how it impacts on communication and how it's fluid in communities).

For *'Technology'* we explore *collaboration* (raising performance, supporting each other to succeed), looking at social technology and understanding the dynamics of how we co-create meaning, we look at the notion of *Social Capital* (to survive and thrive in the Social Age) and how leaders need to help build and share it, and we explore *co-creation* through facilitating technologies (how we create meaning together and the role of this in asynchronous environments). Technology is also about how this is facilitated and how we ensure nobody is left behind.

Social Leaders need to understand and master all three Dimensions.

There are common themes: Narrative runs through everything, through three levels. There is *personal narrative*, our individual learning, there's the *co-created narrative*, forged in social spaces and communities, and there's *organisational narrative*, the story of change that the organisation narrates. The three are interlinked (you can read more about these three levels in Part 3).

Reputation and authority are also deeply embedded throughout: reputation is founded upon curatorial skills, forged in communities and facilitated by technology.

For each component I'm also showing an outer layer, with some specific tools and concepts that can be explored further. This layer is likely to continue developing: as Harold Jarche says, we're in constant beta. Specifically, I'm developing some online diagnostic tools to look at capability in some areas.

What we end up with, then, is a journey from the centre circle, which is a conceptual view defining the three Dimensions, through to the nine components, which define specific skills, and then out to the actual diagnostics and tools to use in the workplace.

I should reiterate: Social Leadership is not a replacement for formal authority. It complements it. Or subverts it, when formal leadership fails. And fail it does. The mission of the Social Leader is to create a highly successful business, successful by all the usual metrics of success. Profit. Attraction of great talent. Retention. Low rates of churn. Innovation. But also a business that is better: led with humility, kindness, fairness. Led by people who strive for equality and fight for it when needed. People who engage with respect and earn the respect of others. A Social Business that earns its right to succeed.

To master a more Social model of Leadership, we need first to understand the context of the Social Age, then we need to master specific technical and social skills to be successful. This book will cover both these elements, exploring the realities of work and life in the Social Age and a practical model for developing leaders.

The 1st Dimension of Social Leadership: Narrative in the NET Model

Narrative is about understanding how we communicate in stories, about how we can shape and influence these to be effective leaders in the Social Age. It covers the way we find things out, the ways we interpret them, the ways we share that information in stories and how we interact with other people whilst we do so.

We communicate in stories, building personal stories, co-created group stories and high-level organisational ones. There is a common *'Narrative'* that crosses all three of these boundaries. As Social Leaders, we need to understand how we narrate our personal story, how we develop that in teams into a co-created narrative, and how that relates to and shapes the overall organisational narrative. Narratives are fluid, evolving over time and in response to circumstances, but they are not out of our control: we have the ability to shape and influence them.

Curation focuses on three states: *discovery, perception* and *interpretation*. Discovery is about how we find things out, perception is about seeing the structure, and interpretation is about finding the meaning, contextualising it to our reality. Curation is an active skill, not a passive one: it's about identifying gaps in skills and knowledge and plugging them, but also about building communities and networks. Curation is a continuous process, forming a foundation for the stories we tell.

> *Practical: The practical activities that will relate to curation are around knowledge-management methodologies, around filtering and around unconscious bias.*

Within the storytelling component of Social Leadership, we are looking at how stories work, about shape, structure, tone of voice and interconnection (how they relate to other stories). We need to understand the theory of storytelling, exploring how stories contain information and how that information is structured and perceived, in order to develop coherent narratives, stories that make sense in isolation and when connected to our individual realities.

> *Practical: The practical activities that will relate to storytelling include practising different stances, exploring how stories convey meaning and crafting messages from multiple viewpoints, moving the location of the story.*

Sharing is about inward- and outward-facing realities and reciprocity. Later we will cover the social technologies that facilitate sharing, but for now we are interested in how relationships are reinforced through sharing, the differences between synchronous and asynchronous sharing and how sharing is a differentiating skill in the Social Age.

> *Practical:* Activities to develop sharing skills would include mapping a communication strategy, looking at perspectives and scheduling.

Narrative is the first Dimension of Social Leadership: it's about how we curate our knowledge and skills, how we understand our boundaries and limitations and how we tell meaningful, engaging stories to effect change. Narrative forms a foundation for Engagement and is facilitated by Technology.

The 2nd Dimension of Social Leadership: Engagement in the NET Model

The realities of leadership are changing: positional authority is being subverted by reputation, built in communities. For this reason, Social Leaders have to be more agile, more able to respond to the synchronous dialogues of the Social Age, able to connect in communities and reciprocate effectively. Social Leadership is very much about actions in the moment, within a mindset that develops reputation over time.

Community is the reality of the Social Age: we come together in communities to learn, to explore, to challenge and to co-create shared meaning. Communities may be emergent and short lived, formed around specific challenges or projects, or they may be personal learning networks that travel with us throughout our careers. Communities may be entirely social or completely formal: they are often specialist and we belong to and contribute within a wide range.

Not all communities are the same: learning communities tend towards more structure, a scaffolded approach to discussion, whilst fully social ones are less structured, happy to move with the trends. Social Leaders need to be able to engage within communities with humility and consistency: they need to develop a tone of voice that helps build reputation, but reputation will be formed on quality of curation and storytelling, skills we explore under *Narrative*.

Social Leadership skills around community are about participation and creation; Social Leaders sometimes take part in active communities, but also need to be able to form spontaneously emergent communities around specific challenges, drawing upon their reputation to build and sustain these. Social Capital is a key concept, and developing this in others a key skill.

> *Practical: Exercises around mapping communities and our participation within them, developing Social Capital in others and around tone of voice for Engagement. Moderation skills and an understanding of the lifecycle of communities are also valuable.*

In the Social Age, reputation is vital and it's under our control: reputation is founded upon our actions, our responses, our tone of voice and stance. It's built – forged – in real time within our communities, and a strong reputation is the hallmark of a good leader. Reputation in the Social Age is based upon our ability to create meaning and to help others to do the same: it's usually less about knowledge, more about agility, the skills to find things out and synthesise those things into an interpretation, creating new meaning. Then taking action: reputation is about getting things done and supporting others as they do the same.

In the Social Age, humility and sharing are key reinforcers of reputation, recognising the agile nature of work and roles within teams. Indeed, I've often said that Social Leadership is a fluid role, defined by the moment, not by a job title: good Social Leaders will sometimes pass the baton on when circumstances warrant it. It's contextual and consensual. One of the greatest skills of a Social Leader is to set aside their mantle of leadership.

> *Practical: Exercises around narration, stance, authenticity and tone of voice help us to think about reputation. Developing skills to understand the role of reciprocity.*

The nature of authority is changing: it's less about positional, hierarchical authority, more about reputation-driven impact. Newer models are subverting the old. The Social Leader needs to recognise the source of their authority (through developing reputation) and be effective at using that power (through honing Narrative and community skills).

The foundations of authority in the Social Age are within community: it's this grassroots connection that allows Social Leaders to be truly agile, to deploy their networks in support of change, indeed, to welcome change (because they recognise that change is constant and presents opportunities).

> *Practical: Models of authority and recognising our style, self-diagnostics to map areas of influence, developing agility in forms of response, influence and contracting with teams.*

The Engagement Dimension of Social Leadership is all about connecting with communities and teams and delivering change. Reputation gives us authority, grounded within community. Engagement is where things happen. It's the thing most desired by organisations and the thing that can only be built on integrity and humility in the Social Age.

The 3rd Dimension of Social Leadership: Technology

Technology isn't about software and code, but rather about how Technology facilitates community building, delivers experiences. We're looking at how Social Leaders need to use Technology to foster and support Narrative and Engagement, looking at how the first two Dimensions are facilitated by the third.

Social Leadership is inherently collaborative: it's about communities. Social Leaders need to recognise the function of communities and support their establishment (in agile ways around challenges and projects), as well as understanding their role and the processes of moderation and support. The role of Technology in communities is largely around facilitation and dissemination: our PCs, smartphones and iPads provide access whilst we are on the move, meaning a shift towards more synchronous Engagement in dialogue. *'Little and often'* is the order of the day: collaborative learning spaces are not deeply reflective, but they are partially so.

The value is more in the dialogue and the sharing than in thinking of it as your life's work (there are exceptions, but broadly I see these collaborative community spaces as conversations with an extra dimension added). There is more room to think than in a straight conversation, but the meaning is still emergent from the group, it's not the highly reflective space of a book or article. They rely on a pace of dialogue, on the speed and responsiveness of conversation.

Collaboration is about forming mutually beneficial relationships, but the benefits may not be synchronous: you build credit against your reputation that may be cashed in later. Collaboration takes place within communities, but the existence of a community does not guarantee collaboration: it needs to be fostered. When this is done using Technology, it differs from *'in the real world'*, and that's why *'community'* falls under Engagement, but *'collaboration'* sits within Technology. We have to understand the tools at our disposal.

Within Technology, we need to explore methods for understanding and mapping collaboration, strategies for collaboration and how people engage and form relationships. It's about understanding reciprocity. Understanding these foundations lets us more effectively structure our interventions and inputs, helping us derive maximum value.

Collaboration falls under Technology because I'm particularly interested in how we use Technology to remain engaged with those groups whilst we are on the move, whilst we are within our everyday reality rather than the abstract classroom or workshop.

Practical: Community mapping exercises and ways of characterising modes of interaction within those spaces, as well as strategies for Engagement in an agile way. Methods for assessing which spaces to use to support new communities and how Technology can facilitate our leadership style.

Social Capital is one's ability to survive and thrive in collaborative online communities: it's about success in Engagement, about safeguarding people against mistakes and about preventing anyone being disenfranchised through skill or Technology. It's part of the role of the Social Leader to have high Social Capital, but also to utilise a range of methodologies to develop this in others.

Trust and integrity are important concepts in the development of Social Capital: relationships are based on these but, in the Social Age, where personality is projected into virtual spaces, things are not as clear as you might think. Social spaces are not independent of context: what will my employer think, what will my friends and colleagues think, what are the consequences of conversations? Social Leaders have to have the skills to ensure that nobody is left behind, to ensure that collaboration is fostered through great conversations and narratives, not controlled through policies and punishment. Collaboration relies on trust, clarity and fairness.

Practical: We have to explore methodologies for building Social Capital (as well as identifying exclusion and addressing it). Recognising disenfranchisement and strategies for Engagement. Identifying what's 'fair' and incorporating that into our decision making.

The co-creation of meaning is one of my favourite topics: it's about how we come together to learn, and it ties in with other areas I've explored previously around music and storytelling. When we learn, we create meaning out of knowledge, out of what we find out. Meaning is personal, contextual, time limited and evolving: it's created in the moment and moves over time. I'd argue that we have moved away from forms of static meaning, towards more fluid, adaptive and dynamic models.

Within groups, we go through a process of co-creation, where consensus is reached and methodologies applied to deal with dissent. In the Social Age, this conversation takes place in real spaces as well as online communities and within our networks, through synchronous and asynchronous conversations. Understanding the process, being able to facilitate and participate in the co-creation of meaning is a key Social Leadership skill.

It's about understanding how people come together to make sense of the world around them, how we cope with and thrive on change, how relationships are formed and evolve and how we respond to new inputs as a group. It's the living, breathing heart of how organisations work: creating meaning together. This is what shapes organisational culture and thinking.

As with collaboration, our Technology focus here is on understanding the realities of how this works in the Social Age, facilitated by Technology, but all about people.

> *Practical: Exercises in co-creation, understanding roles within communities (subject matter, information, validator, narrator, etc.), flexibility in role and stance in community, negotiating responsibly.*

The Nine Skills of Social Leadership

Now that we've seen an outline of the three Dimensions, it's time to delve into the detail of the nine core skills that sit underneath them.

1st Dimension: Narrative

Component 1: Curation in Social Leadership

The 1st Dimension in the NET Model of Social Leadership is Narrative. Curation is one part of this, and it's to do with how we shape our presence, how we curate our reputation and our selves in the world around us.

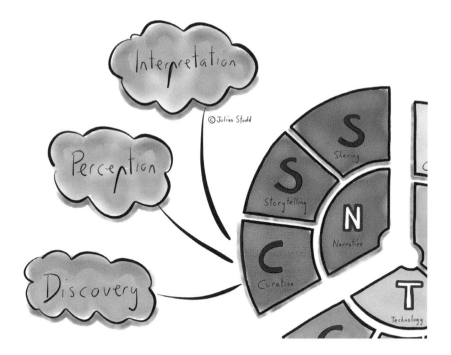

Curation focuses on three states: discovery, perception and interpretation. Discovery is about how we find things out, perception is about seeing the structure, and interpretation about finding the meaning, contextualising it to our reality. Curation is an active skill, not a passive one: it's about identifying gaps in skills and knowledge and plugging them, but also about building communities and networks. Curation is a continuous process, forming a foundation for the stories we tell.

We can view *curation* as taking control of something we do naturally: we all curate our presence, whether we think about it or not. What shoes you wear, how your hair is cut, what car you drive, who you send birthday cards to: these are all curatorial acts. As we define our personas, create the spaces that we live and work in, then we also fill in the gaps: we learn new skills, buy new clothes, make new contacts to expand and shape our lives in specific ways.

In a museum, the curator has many responsibilities: they find and bring new artefacts into the collection, with an eye on the value of that object in isolation, but also in the context of the rest of the collection. An original Apple Macintosh computer may be nice in isolation, but in the context of a display showing the complete sequence of development through to the iPad today, it has greater value. Context is everything.

One aspect to be aware of is bias in curation: as people become increasingly socially aware and connected within communities, we can start to see a high volume of sharing, but there may be bias within what's shared. Is everything from *Harvard Business Review*, or other North American sources? Is it all from middle-aged men? Diversity is a strength for the Social Business, in its people, its thinking and its curation.

But it's not enough to just have something within the collection: we have to be able to identify and articulate the value. We have to be able to interpret it within a context for the recipient (which I'll cover in more detail around *interpretation* in due course...).

In the NET Model, we explore three facets of curation: *discovery*, *perception* and *interpretation*. This is really about how we find things out, how we make sense of them and how we share them, adding context.

Discovery is about placing a stake in the ground and identifying what actions you will take to support that space: what space will you claim as a leader? Do you specialise in particular areas, such as technical project management, legal or operations, or are you a generalist? Do you specialise around projects or around developing teams? In the Social Age, agility is key, but we will also each curate areas of specialism. You need to lay some foundations for reputation as a Social Leader, and once you have done this, you can start to fill in the gaps.

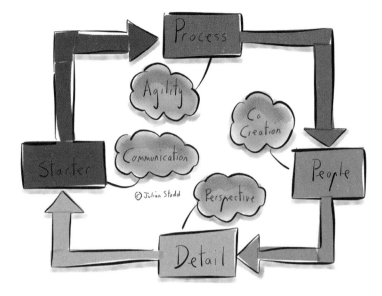

I'm prototyping this format as a structure for this diagnostic exercise: it's a reflective exercise to think about where you add the most value. Are you all about ideas? Are you a starter? Are you about the detail, do you put the structure in place? Are you about people, forming and deploying teams, inspiring and supporting? Or are you about process and compliance, controlling costs and timescales? You probably do a bit of all of these, but where do you see your strengths? They are all aspects of agility.

If you are a *starter*, you need to discover how to be a superb communicator. If you are all about the *detail*, you need to understand perspective. If you are for *people*, then facilitating co-creation is key, and in *process*, it's about agility in the Social Age. As an exercise, individuals would work to determine their perceived strengths, then think about how to discover communities and skills to reinforce these.

What does this mean?

1. What we share impacts on how people perceive us: we have control over this.

2. It's not just what you share, but how you contextualise it that counts.

3. Quality trumps quantity: make it relevant and it's more likely to be amplified.

How can you develop these skills?

1. Rehearsal: you need to find your authentic tone of voice.

2. Learn your strengths: are they aligned with how other people see you?

3. Cultivate strong networks that specialise in specific areas: you are not alone, you need community to curate effectively.

Component 2: Storytelling in Social Leadership

Social Leadership is about ethical decision making and acting with integrity and transparency to deliver the promises of a new Social Contract, where employer and employee both need to find value.

Storytelling is a nuanced activity: it's worth deconstructing it to explore the components.

We communicate in stories: establishing commonality and sharing values. From the earliest stories warning us against wandering off alone at night or why we need to be wary of strangers, through to tales of nation building and love, stories are the units in which we create and share meaning.

Cultures build their histories around stories, but stories are not truth: they are an interpretation, flavoured and coloured by our preconceptions, our history, viewpoint and context. Stories are intensely personal but highly subjective.

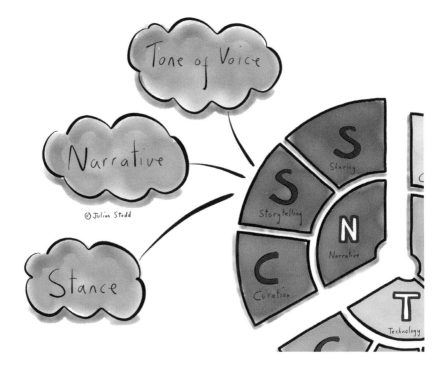

© Julian Stodd

Within Social Leadership, I use three components for Narrative: *curation*, *storytelling* and *sharing*. Curation, as we've seen, is about determining the content for your stores, it's about curating the space that you will be known for and determining what will add value as opposed to cluttering up the airwaves. Storytelling involves us determining how to create meaning around the content.

Stories require some structure: we need to consider our stance, our characters, our tone of voice and overall story length, as well as the genre we use and where the bookmarks go.

No learning happens in isolation, so the context for storytelling within an organisation is important: where is your story coming from, is it *'official'* or *'informal'*, am I expected to act upon it or just enjoy it? As Social Leaders, we need to be able to actively choose the styles of our stories and illustrate them accordingly. Formal stories need a particular structure, whilst informal ones may vary. Our stance is the viewpoint from which we start: are we *alongside* the learner, or are we standing in front of them and explaining things? Are we being directive and telling them that *'this is what the story is'*, or are we co-creating the meaning alongside them?

We fill our lives with books, but don't use all of them all the time: when choosing to read with my favourite nephew, I choose a particular storybook (a Thomas the Tank Engine one, of course), whilst for my niece it's different (frustratingly reinforcing gender stereotypes by being largely pink and involving fairies and ballet). The genre, characterisation, style and length all impact on likely engagement.

Of course, we are not writing novels for our teams, but the principles of what make stories stick are the same: well crafted, coherent, emotionally engaging, free from spelling mistakes!

We also need a good balance of the factual and the social, a balance between just pushing out information (which may not be best done through stories) and pure social chatter (which lacks focus). We need to engage but also inform.

Narrative and story: the words can change, but the Narrative remains the same.

It's worth thinking about two elements: Narrative and story.

The Narrative is the core informational structure, the story is the words we put around it. Organisations often focus effort on controlling the story, when the Narrative is more important. The words can change with each retelling, but the Narrative remains the same. It's like the story of the fall of Troy: you can read the original texts, you can read an academic study or a children's book, or you can watch Brad Pitt in the film, but whatever version of the story you experience, the core Narrative is the same. It's just retellings of that Narrative.

Whilst this is a slightly simplistic view, what I want to emphasise is that you don't have to exert effort trying to control the retellings, you just need to work on the strength and coherence of the core Narrative.

Social Leaders propagate the seeds of stories within their communities: they set them free to be told and retold, each retelling grounded in the core Narrative but taking on its own story form. Indeed, the process of curation (with its interpretation and sense making) is largely about the reframing of stories to be appropriate and to resonate with our core audiences.

So here is the foundation of a model for shaping and releasing stories as a true Social Leader!

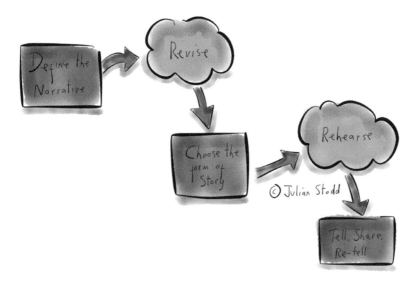

We define a Narrative, choose the story form, then tell and retell the story.

It's iterative: first, define the core Narrative, but don't set it in stone. With each retelling, as well as the passage of time, we revise and strengthen this (through various social and formal spaces). We need to choose the story form and rehearse our telling of it. The process of telling and retelling it is where we refine our messages and our delivery.

What does this mean?

1. Storytelling skills are important: but you need to understand the difference between *story* and *Narrative*.

2. Stance, tone of voice and authenticity all impact on how stories are received.

3. Strong stories may be amplified: weak stories will fall by the wayside.

How can you develop these skills?

1. Take time to reflect on your Narrative and...

2. ...use reflective spaces to refine it.

3. Practise the telling and retelling of core stories to develop your stance and vocabulary.

Component 3: Sharing in Social Leadership

I lent Sam my copy of *Business Model Generation* last week. It's a great book, really useful in getting your thoughts straight in the early stages of planning, so I wanted to share it with him as he is working on business strategy right now.

Cath showed me a video on YouTube last night: *Caravan of Thieves*, a band she saw in America when she was playing at a festival there. She thought I'd like to see them as I'm in the US frequently.

There's a common theme: both Cath and I saw something, thought it was good, and **shared** it with specific people accordingly, based on our knowledge of their likes, needs and interests. We both put a context around what we shared. We both used an appropriate channel to share it in, and it was timely. When we chose what to share, we were aware that our reputation was at stake: if you share a long and tedious book, or a song that I hate, my view of your taste suffers.

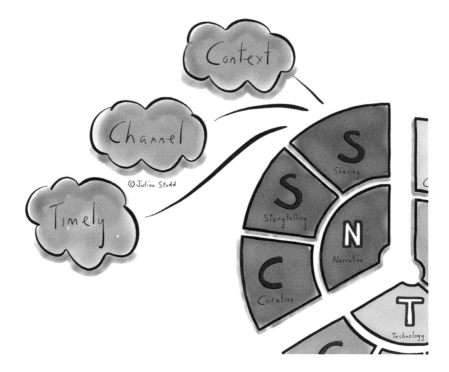

Setting appropriate *context*, choosing the right *channel* and making our shares *timely* are three skills within sharing.

What are we going to share? In the Social Age, the question is more *'what are we going to hide?'*. We share ideas, articles, books, music, we share our time, our feedback, encouragement and support. We share things that make us laugh or make us better. We find the meaning in things and situations and share that too. Sharing is a key skill of Social Leaders because it contributes to reputation, and reputation drives authority. Reputation is ultimately what makes us effective.

Finding context is about identifying where the meaning sits for someone else. What's relevant to me today may be of no interest to you in your current context (but may be highly relevant tomorrow, in your next). To define context, we have to know people: not just their LinkedIn profile and homepage on a corporate intranet, but know them through interaction, through listening and experiencing their reality. Sharing may sound altruistic, but it draws us closer together.

Our contexts are defined by our everyday reality, by the pressures that surround us and the reward mechanisms that pay us, but also by our history and stance: our ethical perspectives and social values. You can't set a context effectively without empathy and understanding. Old-school advertising approaches that work on target audiences are outdated here: we are sharing to individuals, to create personal meaning, not mass audiences. Reputation is built incrementally through this, permeating through the nodes and amplifiers within networks, like the President kissing babies as he heads through the Midwest states.

Amplification occurs through first-, second- and third-order effects: people I know and influence, people connected to those people who, if the first-order influencers have strong reputation, will amplify it. And people who fall ever further out in the network. Influenced by influencers. The portability of our story counts, the persistence of the Narrative, and the quality of our first-order network.

Choosing the channel through which you share is an important decision, impacted by considerations of time, convenience, cost, impact and shared value. Some channels have imbued value: books carry gravitas, LinkedIn is related to businesses and job search, Facebook is more social. These vary by individual (another reason to understand someone's everyday reality). There's no point in me trying to share something with Benoit through Dropbox, because within his corporate reality, it's impossible to access.

Different channels also have different impact: giving someone a book is a tactile as well as an emotionally engaging experience. It's a token, it represents more than just collected words. But if we are talking to busy people, if our team is under pressure, a book may not be very useful: perhaps a link to an article (or even a book review) is more relevant. There's also something to consider about what we are sharing and how suitable each channel is for the format and subject matter: reading text on mobiles is tedious, watching videos takes bandwidth, performance support materials should be concise and clear, easy to digest in seconds, not hours.

Conversely, sharing stories that the organisation passes onto us, stories which have low authenticity or credibility, will actively damage our reputation. Or damage the authenticity of our messaging.

And don't forget the time: shares can be time critical for different reasons. Sometimes the knowledge expires – telling someone about an event or meeting, for example. Sometimes knowledge or shares decay over time: an article may date over a year or two, especially if it relates to technology! Sometimes the timeliness relates to the individual we are sharing with: they may be searching for a new job or facing a specific challenge. Indeed, perceptive Social Leaders will aim to share relevant material within an appropriate context to support people at exactly these times.

Sharing may be about sharing our time: this is where we are sharing our thoughts or ideas and, again, the timing of this may be valuable for us (as we refine and iterate our ideas through our communities, much as I'm doing right now in this draft) and for whoever we share with (where we may trigger thoughts for them too). Sharing is very much a co-creative experience.

What does this mean?

1. Sharing bolsters reputation: it's about quality, context, relevance and timeliness, not volume.

2. Sharing must be in line with your curated space: if you catch me sharing stories about football, it's incongruous.

3. Where you share is as important as what you share: are you up to date with the ecosystem of the Social Age?

How can you develop these skills?

1. Explore the channels you can share in: see what other people do and form your sharing plan.

2. Consciously consider context and timeliness.

3. Take time to get to know people better: use that knowledge to share wisely.

2nd Dimension: Engagement

Component 4: Community in Social Leadership

The Social Age is about communities: communities that are no longer defined by purely physical or geographical borders. Today, our communities crisscross the world, our membership and conversations facilitated by Social Collaborative Technology and shared through the amplification of ideas. Social Leaders need to understand where these communities exist, how to engage in them and how to utilise them to lead effectively.

Unlike in more traditional leadership models, leadership in the communities of the Social Age is through authority based on reputation, not hierarchy. In other words, leadership is earned, not bestowed. The power is consensual.

We start by looking at location. How many communities are visible, how many hidden? A community may be formal and internal, for example, a group of colleagues conversing on a Yammer or intranet forum, or it may be formal and external, such as a professional discussion on LinkedIn. Membership may be entirely drawn from an employed population (typical for an intranet), a combination of employed and contractors, or almost entirely external, beyond traditional organisational control or view. Communities based around professional challenges may fall into this category, such as a community of global project managers or people who are interested in research on unconscious bias.

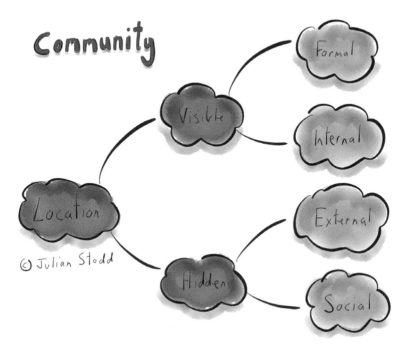

Different communities have different types of conversations and, as a rule, the further away they get from the formal space, the less under the influence of the organisation they are. It's not that organisations can't engage in these conversations: it's just that they have to recognise the semi-formal nature of the environment. In the Social Age, the meaning and conversations are co-owned and co-created by communities, not owned and imposed by organisations. That's why Social Leaders have to understand the ecosystem, and engage in, or phrase, conversations accordingly.

Communities serve different purposes: Social Leaders need to understand the different purposes of different communities and adopt an appropriate stance and style as a result. Communities are used for sense making, for creating meaning, in Social Age terms, but they are not always about sharing ideas we already understand. They may be about enlightenment: bringing new knowledge and ideas to the members. Within a community, different people will be enlightened in different areas and Social Leaders need to understand where they curate their position and act accordingly.

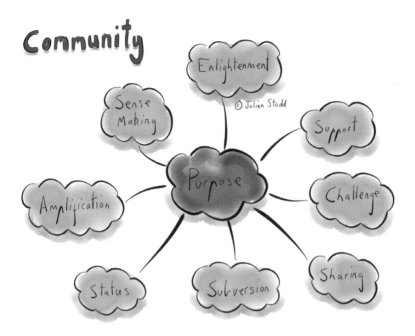

Communities are used for support and challenge, which are flip sides of the same coin. When we bring ideas or problems to a community to resolve, we can expect both support and challenge. It's this very process that gives community sense making such value.

Communities can also be used to subvert existing wisdom: this subversive nature of communities is important for agile businesses, because they rely on the subversive process to be creative, to be innovative. Existing processes give existing results, and sometimes we have to break things to reiterate them in a better frame. But leaders engage in these subversive spaces carefully: the mantle of leadership counts for nothing in subversive spaces, and may indeed be a hindrance.

Some communities give us status, such as professional bodies or exclusive clubs for supporting change. Again, Social Leaders need to understand their terms of engagement in these spaces and may indeed want to create these spaces themselves. Building your own exclusive community for subversives or change agents may be a powerful way of mobilising the semi-formal channels in support of your individual and organisational goals. I've been working alongside some Healthcare Radicals groups within the NHS who are doing exactly this: they are subversive, but fully supported by leadership.

If you're particularly interested in how Communities can be used to drive change, you may enjoy my work on the Dynamic Change Framework, which explores how we create and use external Change Spaces, communities with a space and permission to co-create and co-own change... but that's another story. If you are interested in Organisational Change for the Social Age, come and find me on the blog at www.julianstodd.wordpress.com and I'll share it with you.

Finally, communities can be powerful amplifiers, and amplification is a core feature of the Social Age: understanding how ideas and stories are amplified enables us to be heard more widely without shouting more loudly. It's about creating and sharing magnetic stories: sharing wisely.

So what's your role within these communities?

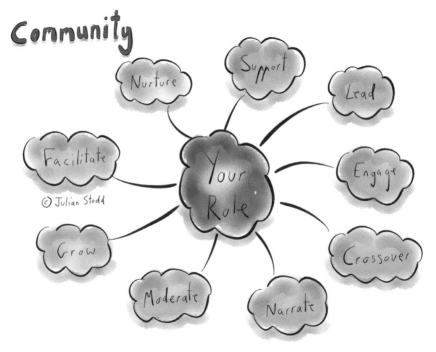

Within our communities, we take many different roles: they are contextual and fluid over time.

We can identify nine functions of the role: to *nurture* individuals and ideas, to *support* the community, to *lead* it in certain areas, to *engage* in other conversations, to *crossover* between communities and share wisdom, to *narrate* the stories that are told, sometimes to *moderate* conversations, to *grow* the community, and to *facilitate* change.

With limited time and resources (not to mention emotional energy), Social Leaders need to plan how they engage. We don't want to get stuck in one segment: too much time moderating may be at the cost of nurturing. Too much growth is no good if we aren't getting value by sharing great stories (although conversely, great stories will generate growth, or they will if we share them widely with amplifiers... it's a great circular process!).

So let's join it together to look at how Social Leaders should approach community: they need to map the communities to understand the ecosystem of Engagement. Once they've determined where the communities are (both the formal and the social ones) they can decide on the purpose of each, which will impact whether and how they engage and what role they take (recognising the need to be agile in role over time). Once we're engaged in communities, we pause to reflect on what we gain through membership and, in time, narrate those stories back out into our communities. That's a truly social way of working.

Community is the fourth of the nine skills of Social Leadership. We've looked at it in terms of *location*, purpose and role to establish rules for how and why we engage and what we can expect to get out of it.

What does this mean?

1. Communities are the source of reputation, and hence, authority, in the Social Age.

2. They are sense-making entities, but we have to learn how to engage effectively.

3. The purposes that communities serve and our roles within them are fluid: we should seek to understand this to be effective.

How can you develop these skills?

1. Map your communities and reflect on the purpose each serves: do you have access to the right expertise?

2. Consider your role: are you fluid in your stance and approach. Do you have the right skills when you need to listen?

3. Consciously and constantly review your communities and your approach to working with them: that's agility.

Component 5: Reputation in Social Leadership

We've covered foundations, but now it's the hard stuff: Social Reputation and Social Authority. One gives the other, but in the Social Age, traditional foundations of authority are subverted by more social and fluid forms.

Reputation is not a matter of marketing: it's a matter of actions and intentions. More specifically, the actions that are born of intentions. You can be full of good intentions, but if your actions don't match or exceed them then you're not a Social Leader. You're probably falling back on more traditional forms of power.

Power: where does it come from?

There are different forms of power, sources of authority. Positional power is the most obvious form of authority: power based in hierarchy and structure. It's the type of power that we codify in institutions and systems and it's the least fluid of them all. There is often a view that hierarchical power is necessary in certain situations, when things need to be decided fast or where clear allocation of risk and responsibility is needed, but this is outdated.

Communities are great sense-making spaces, but they don't divest us of individual responsibility. Social approaches don't require us to abandon formal hierarchies, but they do require us to recognise that our hierarchical power may be matched by socially derived forms, based around reputation.

Subject-matter expertise is another form of power: simply knowing more than someone else about something (be it nuclear fusion or how to operate the office photocopier). We all derive some of our power through subject-matter expertise: it sits within normal social dynamics and powers our stories and conversations. But only the lethargic will rely on their expertise as a foundation for their power in the Social Age, when meaning is what counts, the ability to create meaning based on knowledge. We can easily be left behind if we anchor our reputation to knowledge in the growing storm.

As our relationship with knowledge evolves, so too does the way in which pure knowledge informs reputation and authority.

We see this in healthcare right now: we used to go to the doctor to find out what was wrong with us and to make us better. Today, increasingly, people are accessing pure knowledge online and through communities and turning up to see their doctor with an initial self-diagnosis and even an expectation of treatment. This doesn't make the role of the doctor redundant. Far from it: it changes it from one of pure source of knowledge to practitioner based on ability to join the dots, to work with broad knowledge and experience. Experience is more than knowledge: it's the benefit of multiple stories, the ability to effect change, to impact through action.

Indeed, as knowledge evolves, I speak to doctors who not only are used to patients turning up with diagnostic data from wearable tech, with research they have found, but also from research they have commissioned, in patient groups, themselves. The democratising power of the Social Age means that knowledge is no longer owned by the elite: it can be crowd sourced and created in communities, freely sourced and shared.

Longevity is a source of power: someone who has done something for a long time or who has been in role forever. This is risky, though: where the Social Age rewards agility, there is a risk that longevity alone simply means that you are becalmed by familiarity. That wouldn't be an issue if the world was static, but in fact it's changing around our ears, and solutions or approaches that worked a year ago may not work now. Agility is the ability to create meaning in the moment and to respond to the change.

We need to reflect on sources of power to see how they are changing as a function of wider changes in society (facilitated by technology).

Reputation is a measure of our standing, a measure of how the community values our input: the greater your reputation, the more you can influence on a particular subject, but also the more willing the community is to tolerate your mistakes. This notion around mistakes is important, especially as formal systems are often somewhat intolerant of failure. If social systems are more willing to provide space to learn, they will inherently continue to grow stronger.

When looking at reputation, we can consider three stages that allow us to take a more active control: *navigate, respond, evaluate*.

It's part of actively curating our reputation: to chart a course through all possible actions, recognise when we are responding through habit and reflect on that to see what source of power we are drawing upon, respond to the triggers to moderate our response and then evaluate the effectiveness of that response and quantify how it enhances reputation. Finally, we reflect and narrate, staples of *'working out loud'*, a reflective approach to developing capability.

Let's look at these in more detail.

Navigation is a mindset: out of all possible courses of action, which one will we take, and are we being pushed there by the current or actively choosing the route?

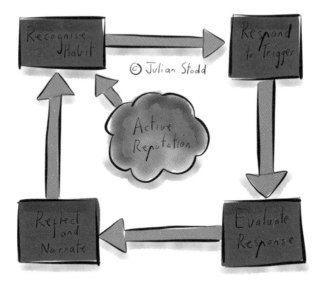

We are creatures of habit, which makes us effective (because we efficiently deal with recurring situations with the minimum of thinking required) but also lethargic (because we often fail to evolve our responses and to act with agility, testing out new problem-solving methods). Habits are neurologically efficient, and effective, but we need to reflect on their appropriateness. Indeed, just recognising when we are responding through habit and when through conscious decision making is valuable.

Once we understand our reliance on habit, we can determine our *triggered responses*: the reason this is important is because triggered responses reinforce reputation, so if we never reflect upon and adapt our responses, we will forever be caught within our current reputation.

Because the Social Age is about creating meaning within the moment, it's about action review cycles, testing new approaches and being unafraid to modify them. It's about agility.

Evaluating responses ensures that we are taking a learning approach, not just firing solutions out into the world and hoping for the best. Responses within communities are far easier to evaluate, because the community provides a narrative, it gives us real-time feedback.

Evaluation ties in with notions of amplification: as we learn what works, what reinforces our reputation and makes our stories more effective, we should do more of it.

Finally we *reflect* and *narrate*, this being a staple of the Social Age. Reflection is about measuring impact and gauging our learning, it's about inward reflection (how have I changed?) and outward reflection (sharing the story of your learning). We then narrate our learning to the community, to share both the good and the bad, the things we got right and the parts we got wrong. This narrative is an open and honest approach to leadership and directly contributes to our reputation.

Social Leaders need a strong reputation in both formal and social spaces. They need to be adept at *'playing the game'* within the formal spaces (having data-driven conversations, influencing, building formal authority), but also at social approaches (challenging and supporting, even subverting inefficient processes and controls). They have to play both games.

We see this with the emergence of the socially active leaders: the blogging and tweeting CEO who is #WorkingOutLoud and directly visible to the community (contrast that with the hierarchical CEO who hides in an ivory tower and rarely meets employees or customers directly on his or her journey from BMW to the lift to the top floor).

The other key facet of reputation is its link to fairness, equality and kindness, not as peripheral, incidental, accidental things, but as a core of how we behave, what our role as a leader is.

Social Leaders do the things that are right, not just the things that they are told to do, or have to do. They do what's right, even when it brings them into conflict with the system, because they recognise that if the system conflicts with what's right, it's the system that is at fault. They open up conversations, offer constructive challenge and offer to work together to change it. If it comes to it, they side with what's right, because that's where their reputation takes them.

Reputation subverts other forms of authority but may, if built well, complement them. We can have the best of both worlds if we are able to understand what each can give us and be true to both.

What does this mean?

1. Reputation subverts older forms of power, such as positional or hierarchical ones.

2. It's forged in social spaces, through actions, not intentions.

3. We need to reflect on our responses: are they through habit or by design?

How can you develop these skills?

1. Learn to recognise habit and the impact it has on reputation.

2. Develop active reputation-management strategies.

3. Learn to effectively narrate your learning, which will build your reputation.

Component 6: Authority in Social Leadership

We could view authority as the goal of Social Leadership. Or, rather, we could if we remained anchored in twentieth-century notions of leadership. Authority is not the goal, but it is a means to an end. If we have authority, we are better able to engage in certain communities, and our messages carry more weight and are more likely to be amplified (if we curate our space well and tell magnetic stories). Authority in the Social Age is founded upon reputation, forged within our communities.

I need to provide some context here: Social Leadership is not intended to replace other forms of leadership. It's complementary. It just carries leadership over, out of purely formal contexts and into the semi-formal spaces that surround them. If we rely on formal, hierarchical forms of power and authority, we limit our influence to formal organisational spaces. At a time when meaning is created in communities – semi-formal, crossing boundaries and geographies – forms of power rooted in the formal have limited appeal and leverage.

Social Leadership requires Engagement, based on trust and integrity. Once we move away from purely formal spaces, boundaries can become unclear. We are creating permissive environments for conversation without always clarifying what types of conversations we will permit. This ambiguity introduces risk for everyone (risks that we may not even realise we have adopted). For example, we create a social collaborative forum and ask people to share ideas for how we can improve the reputation of the business. Someone shares a story about a project they worked on that went wrong and what they learnt from it. At their annual performance review, someone produces this data as evidence of their failed project. Is that fair?

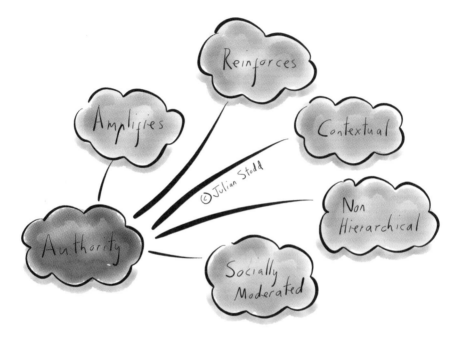

Any notion of authority in Social Leadership needs to take into account these constraints and considerations: the territory can be unclear. Good Social Leaders navigate it, but also help others to do so.

Amplification is a building block of authority, but it relies on this trust being in place: the integrity of any community is founded upon it. Without trust, we cannot effectively engage in a relationship space (although we may engage at a transactional level). Transactional engagement is simply going through the motions, doing what we think is required of us.

This, incidentally, is probably how much organisational training happens. Going through the motions without authenticity, because the risk of opening up is too great.

Authority is based upon your reputation, which is earned from actions over time, which is why Social Leadership is about what you do as much as what you say. The stories you tell and the stories that are told about you. Specifically, it's about the consistency of actions over time: erratic responses erode trust.

Because the authority of Social Leadership is earned, it helps us to amplify our messages, to gain greater traction, which is stronger than the brute force approach that underlies formal hierarchies.

Strong, socially mediated authority reinforces our ability to be effective: in Social Age terms, it reinforces our ability to create meaning within and alongside our communities. This sense-making function of communities is highly valuable: co-creative and co-owned, built from the cognitive surplus and investment of many people.

One of the areas of Social Leadership that can be most challenging is its contextual quality. Whilst within one community I may have authority, in another, I have none. Or, indeed, at a different time within the same community my authority may vary, not because my reputation is damaged, but simply because communities serve different purposes at different times, so leadership (and, indeed, all the other roles) can be contextual. This is one reason why humility is a central trait in Social Leaders: they are willing to put down the mantle of leadership (or, indeed, have it removed from them for a while) for the wellbeing of the wider community.

This is why I describe Social Leadership as *'socially moderated'*: it always requires permission and framing by the community itself. Anytime we exercise the tools of authority without the permission of community, we are simply falling back on positional authority.

As a side note, it is perfectly possible to have positional authority within community spaces: it's simply the choice of Social Leaders not to exercise that power, to be humble, and to rely on the community conferring different forms of authority.

Social Leadership is an extension of authority, from formal spaces into social ones. It's interesting because, in the Social Age, meaning is created largely in these spaces. They are the gateway to increased creativity and innovation: the lifeblood of agile organisations. We are not abandoning formal authority, but rather extending it, with a different set of skills.

The rise of the Social CEO is an interesting phenomenon in itself: people who exercise the ultimate positional authority and yet set it aside to engage directly with the community. Naturally, our formal authority can carry across in terms of reputation to social spaces, but we can't rely on it. A celebrity may garner a large following from simply being famous, but if their input is inane, it won't grow, amplify or confer authority. Conversely, someone with no claim to fame at all can develop great authority purely in social spaces (through great storytelling and resonance).

Authority is complex, nuanced, contextual. In social terms, it's founded upon reputation (built, in turn, upon curation, storytelling, sharing and engagement in community). We can exercise both formal, hierarchical authority and socially moderated authority, but one does not guarantee (or depend upon) the other. Overall, we exist in an ecosystem where formal authority is losing ground to the socially moderated variety, so understanding authority in terms of Social Leadership is powerful.

This shift in the nature of authority itself is hugely significant: one of the building blocks of the Social Age. Organisations who think it can be countered through hierarchical actions are badly mistaken. It's indicative of the wider balancing of power between the individual and the authority of organisations and governments around them. Within the context of the Social Age, it's always the most authentic and compelling voices that prevail.

What does this mean?

1. Authority is founded upon reputation and it's within our power to generate socially moderated authority.

2. Authority in social spaces is highly contextual and consensual, differing widely from formal authority. It's not power without limits, it's power through permission.

3. Understanding amplification in social spaces is important to build authority and harks back to our work around curation and storytelling.

How can you develop these skills?

1. Develop consistent approaches to build authenticity and authority.

2. Explore the nature of relationship and transactional engagement, and focus on building more relationships.

3. Learn how trust works in social spaces and reflect on how the consistency of our actions impact on trust.

3rd Dimension: Technology

Component 7: Co-Creation in Social Leadership

Co-creation is about the ways we come together in social spaces to create meaning. It's a core Social Age process and we can see it everywhere. Collaborative technology enables us to co-create across wider spaces in synchronous, asynchronous and cross-boundary ways. It allows us to form and grow communities and benefit from their sense-making functions.

© Julian Stodd

We achieve more together than we ever can alone. Social Learning spaces do not just bring us together to share what we have learnt, they bring us together to write a story together. To help understand the co-creative process, I've come up with a map of seven elements, seven ways that we use our social spaces to create meaning: building knowledge through iteration and reflection in a community.

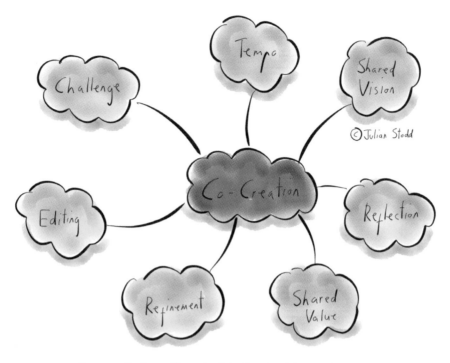

©Julian Stodd

These are the Seven Elements of Co-Creation: it's an exploration
of how we come together to create meaning.

In every village in medieval England was a tithe barn. The tithe was the percentage of the crop that went to the Church and the tithe barn was where it was stored. As with all barns, it had two doors, the front ones very high, the back ones much lower. The fully laden carts came in the front, piled high, then left through the lower doors at the back, emptied. But the doors were not just to facilitate the passage of carts: with both doors thrown open, the space in the middle was breezy, and was known as the threshing floor. The harvested wheat or corn was laid out and beaten with flails, to detach the grains from the heads. The resulting mass was scooped into woven pans, wide, like a scallop shell, and it was thrown into the air. The wind would catch the chaff, the fibrous husk that sits around the grains, and blow it out of the door, letting the grain itself fall back into the woven pan. Repeating this separated the wheat from the chaff.

Harvest and threshing were group activities, where everyone, from young to old, came together to carry out specific tasks. We use Social Learning spaces to refine our messages: to iterate our raw ideas into meaningful actions. To separate out the wheat from the chaff. We do that by throwing our ideas into the wind and seeing what is left behind after the debate. It's how we refine our messages in these spaces. It's part of the co-creative process within the community.

It relates to the wider context of the Social Age: the evolution of knowledge itself, away from something captured and published in a static format, towards something dynamic, co-created and evolved through reflection and application.

Coherent communities, ones that are capable of high functioning, share both purpose and values. They are united in intent, but also united in the values by which they will achieve it. You can impose shared purpose, but shared values have to be found from within.

If the values differ too much, the community fragments into new shapes. Shared value also sits at the heart of communication: we need to share value to understand each other and to develop more refined ideas. Socially collaborative spaces allow us to share value and encourage us to do so by letting us understand the value of other participants. Shared value fosters cooperation and lets us build progressively more complex constructs, based on the foundation values, knowledge and understanding. This is a co-creative process at work.

Part of refining our ideas and narratives in social spaces is that of **editing** things down. We can use social spaces in this function as we rehearse ideas. I've been writing about something called '*co-adaptation*' in music; it's about how two people adapt to match a beat. But my ideas are still raw, my stories unrefined, so I've been rehearsing and editing them all week in various social spaces (from LinkedIn to Yammer and the pub). Each time I tell the story, I get feedback and I refine what I say. The process of editing makes my narrative stronger. As my ideas reach maturity I should be able to edit them to the point that I can explain them concisely and with clarity. This only happens with careful editing and is central to the co-creative processes at play in Social Leadership.

I use a six-step methodology for understanding how we learn. **Reflection** is a key but often neglected part. We need to take the learning and reflect upon it, to stand up the new learning against what we already know to be true, and to develop our thinking accordingly. We may accept or reject new knowledge, but it's an active process that takes reflection. Why have I listed it as a co-creative process? Because reflection is not simply about sitting in a quiet room thinking about whether we believe in something or not. It's an active process that can be embedded in the community. I'm reflecting right now, sitting in a cafe, sharing ideas with people through email, through Twitter, even through Facebook. These very ideas I'm sharing have dedicated time where I'm reflecting on what I'm going to say and I'm refining that message through (and with) my own social communities.

Social Leaders operate in multiple communities, some of which they are a guest in, others of which they may form and lead in more conventional senses. In all of them though, reflection is important, it's part of separating the wheat from the chaff.

Challenge is a vital part of the co-creative process: it's something that is done well, if constructively, in Social Learning and collaborative spaces. We can challenge ideas, argue our case and co-create a shared narrative out of it. The fact is that some of our ideas are strong, some weak, and appropriate challenge helps us to work out which is which. So challenge sits here as one of the seven ways that we use our social community spaces to co-create meaning, to learn, to lead.

Tempo has a role, too: one of the ways to drive up engagement in change is to restrict the length of time that a community space is available, to give it a definite end. This helps drive up the tempo. We can view the range of social media across a spectrum from synchronous to asynchronous. Twitter or forum chatter is often nearly synchronous, virtually conversational. Blogs are more reflective and the shared narrative that we may document and build out of the space tends to be highly asynchronous. It's more broadcast than conversation. It's easy to lose momentum in learning or creative processes. Writing the books has taught me that: I have to dedicate time and share my learning with the community to maintain my own momentum, to get the job done. For those reasons, tempo, the ability to give us momentum and take conversations forward, is included as one of the seven co-creative elements.

Finally, **shared vision**: not the vision of the individual, but rather the shared vision of the community. A desire to learn, to make a difference, a desire to share ideas and do something worthwhile. We come together in these spaces because of the vision, to be inspired by others, as well as to offer inspiration ourselves. It's also about our field of vision being wider with more eyes: more people bringing a wider range of experience, a wider range of sources, creating more wisdom and meaning. The breadth and differences within community make it stronger. Vision inspires us.

So, seven strands of co-creation, seven things we take from social spaces: *refinement*, *shared value*, *editing*, *reflection*, *challenge*, *tempo* and *shared vision*.

Technology enhances and helps narrate the co-creative process: the very permanence that can be problematic in certain circumstances is a benefit in others, particularly in support of knowledge management, building and capturing tribal knowledge and the iterative sense making in communities: as I write this I'm constantly referring back to primary conversations that happened on the blog.

In the midst of our reflection on the co-creative process, there's one thing that's well worth recognising: it's *expressive*. Artistic, almost. Including co-creation within Social Leadership provides an opportunity to draw in our creative and expressive capabilities as well as our strategic and analytical ones. Just as Social Leadership crosses over from social to formal spaces, so too it crosses from analytical to creative ones.

Again, technology plays a role in this through its ability to turn us into producers as well as consumers of content. Whilst formerly, organisational communication was limited to PowerPoints and ClipArt, along with interminable emails and maybe a fax or two, today we communicate through many channels, collaborative shared workspaces, instant messaging and file sharing, using audio, video, mind mapping, drawing and knowledge management and productivity tools like EverNote and Paper by FiftyThree, which is the tool I use for all my illustrations.

What does this mean?

1. Co-creation takes place within our communities: it's a complex process of iteration and review.

2. Co-creation relies on a foundation of trust and integrity: we can nurture the co-creative processes at work in our communities and, indeed, it's important that leaders do.

3. It's a creative as much as technical process: we have to be tolerant of the debate and mistakes as we conduct our sense-making activities.

How can you develop these skills?

1. Explore the seven strands of co-creation: do you recognise them all in your work, or are you missing out?

2. Narrate examples of co-creation to better understand and reflect upon the process.

3. Consider how trust is the foundation of co-creation and develop a plan to support your communities to have clarity of engagement.

Component 8: Social Capital in Social Leadership

With authority comes responsibility: or maybe responsibility drives a need for authority to enable us to do what's right. Social Capital can be defined as our ability to survive and thrive in online social spaces, but it's also about our responsibilities to safeguard others. Leadership in the Social Age is contextual, but always carries a responsibility to be inclusive. It is, after all, Social Leadership, founded within communities. I've become more worried recently that the very technology that permits and enhances collaboration draws ever wider the gap between the socially enabled and the disenfranchised: through poverty, relevance or cultural barriers.

In the old world, the things that kept us apart were poor communications technology and vast distances: in the Social Age, these are gone, replaced instead by lack of equality, lack of opportunity, low Social Capital. People are excluded not so much because they are unable to connect through lack of technology (although that is still an issue), but more because they are not allowed to connect or engage because of their gender, sexual preference or culturally defined status in society.

As we've seen before, communities are based around shared values, shared responsibilities and sometimes a division of labour, but membership is not automatic: it requires certain social skills as well as the right opportunities. Without access to technology, it's hard to be a Social Leader. In societies where the views of minority groups are repressed or ignored, it's hard to build reputation and be part of a community. And forget about it just being minorities: where women are given fewer rights or lower status than men, or where they are prevented from collaborating widely and freely, we can't have effective Social Leadership.

Just as we've talked about the Socially Responsible Business, so too we need to consider the social responsibility of the individual: a responsibility to seek out fairness, to act with humility, to support and promote the views of others and to develop the welfare of the community as a whole.

Remember: it is the role of Social Leaders to do what's right, not just what's legal or compliant. It's their responsibility to change the system where the system fails to be fair.

Social Leaders have high Social Capital themselves: they need to understand the foundations of the Social Age, the realities of the new Social Contract and the underlying technology. They also foster and develop this capability in others. They ensure nobody is excluded through design or by chance. A high moral imperative, you might think, taking us into the realms of Social Justice, not leadership, but why would we aim any lower? There's no such thing as *nearly equal*: if we're not building inclusive communities, if we're not acting with humility, we're not living the values required to be Social Leaders.

Not that you have to be a saint. It's fine to be motivated by money, status or position, you just have to realise that this will exclude you from certain social forms of power (although it may, of course, reinforce other more conventional types).

We can view three elements within Social Capital for our purposes here: *etiquette, humility* and *equality.*

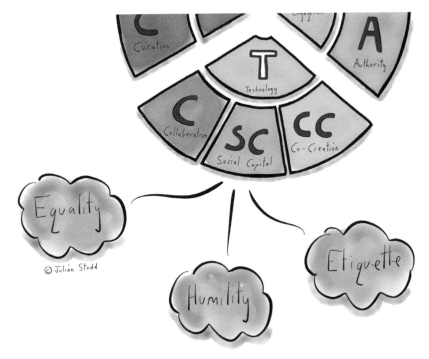

© Julian Stodd

The first, *etiquette*, is, in some ways, the easiest: it's the simple rules of engagement and effectiveness in social collaborative spaces. This ranges from understanding the behaviours we use online (and how they differ from formal organisational spaces, both because they're virtual and because they're social/semi-formal), through to understanding the functioning of things like hashtags and forums at a technical level.

Organisations need to consider actively developing these skills independently of specific projects: we can assume that people know how to access and participate in online communities if we like, but if we don't check, we neglect our responsibilities for inclusion and support. And the rules are complicated because they are not consistent: online social spaces can be complex, hostile, challenging or bemusing, and often all four (they can, of course, be simple, supportive, enriching and engaging, but again, we can't assume this to be true).

Where communities are co-creative and sense making, we have to recognise that roles may be fluid: subject-matter expertise may be as fluid as the conversations themselves. In the Social Age, evolved relationships with knowledge come down more to your ability to find things out than your actual knowledge of things.

Issues of identity and trust also become relevant: identity is more fluid in online spaces and can form a particular hazard as we become unable to compartmentalise conversations effectively if we don't understand who is in them. This compartmentalisation is important because we have to allow communities to form and become coherent in their function, which means building shared value and narrative power, all of which is built on a foundation of trust.

These are big areas to get into, and it's not necessarily the role of Social Leaders to train people, but they must understand the significance and be able to function themselves, to the point where they can diagnose that others are struggling.

Etiquette is about understanding how things work and being able to participate within social (and technical) conventions.

Humility is a mindset around collaboration and co-creation: it's a stance we take in community. It's about recognising the relevance of other views and being willing to set aside our own. Social Leaders are humble because their authority is contextual and consensual, granted by the whim and permission of the community. Social Leadership operates in semi-formal spaces where formal hierarchies of power do not apply. It's not that we can't apply them: we can, of course, assert our formal authority, but that then changes the space into a formal one, not a social one, so the context is lost.

Humility allows us to share effectively: as long as we're prepared to be proven wrong. The point of co-creative spaces is to facilitate the creation of meaning relevant in the moment and the sharing of it through narrative. The point is not to impose our view or dominate the conversation: this would change the space from a collaborative one to a broadcast one, which is what many formal organisational channels become by default. They become about propagating formal organisational stories, not the narratives formed by communities. This ties in with how we organisationally take a stance on moderation and control: it's all very well allowing debate and discussion, but what do we do when we don't like what's said? Especially at times of change, this forms part of the role of Social Leadership: being humble enough to listen in social spaces when people may be disenfranchised or voiceless in formal ones.

Ultimately, I include humility in the model of Social Leadership because of my frustration with egocentric models and with much of the training done around influencing and management, all of which assumes a foundation of formal power and authority for leaders that is simply being eroded in the Social Age. The role of the Social Leader is not one of control through exercise of positional authority: it's one of narrative magnetism, telling stories that are engaging and inclusive and that draw us forwards and together.

Even as I write this, I recognise the idealistic narrative I'm creating: but I believe it's true. To understand how Social Collaborative Technologies allow us to cluster around magnetic ideas, to amplify and extend them, you only have to look at the viral memes that sweep through Facebook on a daily basis. Stories have power: they are magnetic, and a form of leadership grounded in narrative and co-creation can draw upon that power.

Amplification isn't about brute force and older, broadcast, *'push'* models. It's about engagement in depth, throughout multiple communities, about shaping narratives and sharing magnetic stories, filtering out the weaker ideas in our first reflective spaces, developing the stronger ones, curating, sharing. Amplification is a natural force we harness, but with humility: you can't achieve authority for Social Leadership through ego, you can only do it through consensus, within the right context.

The community can grant you the authority, but it can remove it too.

Equality is not something to strive for: it's something to fight for. Odd, maybe, that an act for Social Leaders should be to level the playing field and equalise, but it represents the fact that all voices need to be heard and respected equally.

If we just listen to the vocal or already empowered, we miss the wealth of wisdom and experience from the voiceless and hidden. Plus it assumes or imposes hierarchy in a space that strives for collaboration among equals.

Equality is not easy to achieve: in our shared global culture we experience different legal, ethical and cultural frameworks and we have to respect them, but it's still often clear what's right and what's wrong, and those are the things we have to fight for.

The trouble with fairness is that it doesn't fracture: it's slowly eroded. If we don't respect the people it's easy to respect, how can we hope to be tolerant across the wider gaps. If we don't challenge the laughter on the small things, how can we hope to tackle the really big ones? If equality doesn't start at home, how can we hope to expect it at work, or globally?

For an organisation to tolerate homophobia, racism or discrimination on the grounds of gender or belief is intolerable. It's wrong. When an organisation works globally, it's almost impossible to avoid crossing these cultural boundaries. What's right and true to the given value of *'right'* in my location may be different from what's right and true for the given value of *'right'* in yours. Even if we are unsure how to cross it, we cannot simply ignore it.

The culture is not broken because of one or two people in a remote location: it's broken because of the thirteen other people who laugh along because they don't dare to challenge the laughter. The culture is broken when one person feels like they're disenfranchised for being the one person who is right.

Social Capital is a big area, and every time I revisit it, it gets bigger. But maybe that's because it's so important.

What does this mean?

1. Developing high Social Capital ourselves is about refining our skills whilst remaining humble.

2. It's about drawing everyone together within communities and ensuring that we are fair in what we do and say.

3. Individual Social Capital contributes to an organisation being fair, being equal.

How can you build these skills?

1. The foundation skills of etiquette are mastered through practice and feedback.

2. Humility is gained through reflection: through consistent action over time.

3. Working with a mentor can help with both these things.

4. Equality is about our mindset: exploring unconscious bias can be valuable, but it's also about constantly listening out for the voiceless and addressing disenfranchisement.

Component 9: Collaboration in Social Leadership

The NET Model of Social Leadership is a circle: the ideas and skills it contains live in constant beta, always being refined and adapted as the ecosystem evolves around us. It's not just technology that changes: social attitudes develop, legislation moves on, different voices become louder or less relevant, depending upon their ability to be agile. But, in as far as our journey has a start, a middle and an end (as every good story should), we have reached the final segment.

Collaboration sits at the end of Technology, the third Dimension of the NET Model and we can, to an extent, view it as the pinnacle of Social Leadership. Why? Let's explore:

Social Leaders start by defining their space, taking a stance, looking inwards and finding out what drives and motivates them and what they want to be known for. They learn how to refine their storytelling and communication skills around this core vision and then look to their communities to build reputation and authority. Along the way, they explore the purpose of those communities and their roles within them. Having done so, they seek to develop others, to safeguard them, to include them and ultimately to advance themselves, the organisations and their communities in line with best practice and what's right.

The ability to collaborate widely, to recognise the needs of individuals and organisations and to co-create communities and situations that can serve both is part of the purpose of Social Leadership.

In this sense, collaboration is the peak: to be able to forge fair and productive relationships, to be able to 'make sense' of things, to create (and co-create) meaning and to effectively do that in an inclusive way that gets things done.

But the model is circular for a reason: because the Social Age is also about agility and fluidity: Social Leadership is consensual and contextual and we have to remain relevant. So, as we find our role and exercise our authority (through the permissions of the community), so we must revisit our stance and balance. Have we developed the right skills for today? Do we know the skills we will need tomorrow? Are our communities strong enough, or do we need to enter, create or refine an existing one? Are our teams intact? Or do we need to develop, update or enhance them, either through development or addition (or, indeed, removing someone)? Is our organisation equal? Is it fair? Is it Socially Responsible?

Collaboration is about recognising validity in multiple viewpoints and being willing (and able) to account for them all. It's not about decision making through democratic process: you can still exercise strong and unilateral authority (recognising that it's permissive authority).

Collaboration is a complex process: it's about being fair and productive.
It's about sense making, being inclusive, becoming effective.

Social Leaders should seek to be fair: to do what's right, not just what's covered by process or law. It's about rebalancing the relationship between organisations and individuals to include fairness, a recognition that the needs of both can be reconciled if we are careful. This fairness leads to the ability to better form and participate within communities, communities which make us effective. Because neither membership nor authority is assured, we have to build our own foundations for this, and fairness is a good place to start.

Collaboration is about being productive: productive through being able to get things done, to instigate and carry through change, through collaboratively owned and driven change. It's the co-created and co-owned nature of the Social Age change communities that makes them effective.

We can focus on three elements of collaboration: *'team'*, *'skills'* and *'outcomes'*.

Team is about how Social Leadership, which operates in semi-formal spaces, bridging between the fully formal and entirely social, relates to traditional team structures.

We've explored widely how Social Leaders curate reputation and operate within communities, where their power is consensual, but they also operate within formal teams and often have formal responsibilities to those teams (which may be in conflict with those of their communities). This is the tightrope that Social Leaders have to tread, forever with one foot in the realms of formal hierarchy and authority. It may not always be easy.

Within their formal teams, Social Leaders also conduct sense-making activities.

Engagement in social spaces is highly sensitive to trust, but the types of trust invested in formal hierarchies may be different. Within a formal context, we take it as read that a manager or leader may know things about our circumstances that they can't share with us. In social circles, if a friend withheld information about our wellbeing, we would lose trust. As leaders venture out of the purely formal and into the social, they start to confront these issues.

Social Leadership is still a semi-formal style: it's not devolved from responsibility and regulation. It's a matter of understanding where the challenges lie and approaching them with integrity and clarity.

We see this tension reflected in the wrangling within the HR space as they seek to find relevance in the Social Age: to what extent is HR a mechanism of control and punishment, when rules are flouted, and to what extent is it a facilitating entity that works with the community to evolve those very rules into something more meaningful, all within a framework of fairness.

There's a responsibility on individuals too: we have to accept that information may still be segregated, that Social Leadership approaches are informal but still may cross into certain hierarchies. As I said earlier, it's a balance between how social approaches can complement and reinforce formal ones.

Formal authority alone is not enough.

The mindset of collaborating with our teams rather than leading them through formal authority may be new: it's a magnetic approach to leadership.

We need new skills to collaborate effectively. We've already covered eight of them here, and these skills need to be mastered over time, refined and shared. Under the purview of Social Capital, it's not about learning skills to differentiate us from the crowd: it's about learning skills to share them with the crowd. Old notions of keeping our knowledge hidden away cease to apply in the Social Age: sharing is a differentiating skill and one that we should have mastered by this point, and that applies to skills as well as knowledge.

As we complete our reflection on collaboration, we have to consider outcomes: how effective have we been? Our value depends upon our ability to be more effective, to create meaning and get things done. Collaboration is the platform upon which we can deliver that effectiveness, creating a magnetic leadership approach and co-creating change within our communities and teams, both formal and social.

We can use our new skills around narrative and storytelling to ensure that our success is shared internally, back into formal spaces, as well as socially. It's all part of closing the circle, ensuring that people accompany us on our journey, and it supports the ongoing reputation economy we operate in.

With that in mind, part of our collaborative efforts have to be about reinforcing and growing the reputation and authority of others, by saying thank you, sharing reflections, writing reviews, making recommendations, giving feedback, offering mentoring, coaching others, sharing insights, a continuous process of feeding the community and drawing upon its skills.

What does this mean?

1. Collaboration involves negotiating the space between competing needs and desires of individuals and organisations.

2. The win is to compromise but to be highly effective.

3. Humility may be our greatest strength.

4. We must share outcomes and reflect on our approach, strengths and weaknesses.

5. We need to do so whilst supporting the ongoing development of our teams.

How can you build these skills?

1. We need to address models of negotiation and compromise, developing our skills in these areas.

2. We have to rehearse our narratives of success: how are we building the reputation of others?

3. We must circle around the model to review our other core skills and ensure they stay up to date.

Summary

The journey towards Social Leadership takes us through nine stages: we CURATE our space, choosing the stage we will perform from. We develop our STORYTELLING skills, learning how to structure the Narrative and tell stories that are relevant and timely, interpreting the world around us to create meaning. We SHARE those stories wisely.

Social Leaders work around Engagement to build their REPUTATION, founded upon their stories, and shared in COMMUNITIES, where they actively participate in the discussion. Their AUTHORITY is based upon their reputation, not hierarchy or position.

Social Leaders recognise the facilitating power of Technology and have high SOCIAL CAPITAL, as well as actively developing that in others. They CO-CREATE meaning, recognising that the process of consulting and participating in community makes them stronger, and they COLLABORATE widely, with humility, with no expectation of reciprocity.

Social Leaders are agile, fit for the Social Age. These are skills that we can develop, but they're based on recognising that the fundamental nature of work and learning is changing. We have to master the foundation of the Social Age to be true Social Leaders.

Developing Social Leadership: How do we train it?

In this, the 2nd Edition of the Social Leadership Handbook, I have one key advantage. Prototyping. Some of the ideas in the 1st Edition have now been put into practice. I've had the opportunity to develop theory into practical application, and that's incredibly valuable. Within my own leadership style, I'd be happy to curate a reputation as both a theorist and a practitioner: someone who can develop ideas, but practically implement change. That's my own Social Leadership journey.

If we subscribe to the notion of Social Leadership, and the premise that in the Social Age, we need both styles, formal and social, it leaves us with the challenge of how we develop it. How do we train Social Leadership?

Key to this is understanding that a simple book, like this, or a single workshop is not enough. The journey to becoming a Social Leader is not an intellectual one, it's about lived experience and everyday reality, and so we have to embed our experience within that.

We have to find our own individual journey to being a better Social Leader: it's a journey of discovery, taken (and judged by) our own communities. Success is only assured by action: the developmental framework of the NET Model can be a guide, but it's not something you can be tested formally against. Judgement will lie in the community itself, and in our conscience as we confront it.

The most successful approaches I've worked on have been Scaffolded Social Learning approaches, where we create a series of spaces for individuals to explore topics and build their understanding over time. A small part of this type of journey is formal: explaining concepts and sharing explanations. By far the largest part is experiential, but within a Scaffolding. In this context, the Scaffolding is a structured series of sense-making activities, where individuals bring their everyday reality into the learning community, work on ideas together, and co-create a story around application.

It's a collaborative and evolutionary learning approach. If you're interested in approaches to Scaffolded Social Learning and practical routes to developing Social Leadership, head to the blog, where I constantly #WorkOutLoud and share ideas and reflections on what works and what doesn't!

www.julianstodd.wordpress.com

Part 3: Application

Now that we've explored the foundations of the Social Age and taken a trip through the NET Model of Social Leadership, the third section of this book is about application. It's based around a series of posts from my blog on various applications and contexts for Social Leadership, with some additional commentary added.

Six tenets of Social Leadership

Social Leadership is a style fit for the Social Age: it's about building Social Authority, reputation-based leadership that is consensual by the community. It's complementary to formal leadership but vital at a time when formal authority delivers a diminished return. Here are six tenets that any Social Leader will adhere to:

Be curious: question everything. Just because *'this is how we have always done it'*, don't assume that's how you should continue to do it. Solve for today, remain curious as to tomorrow. Curiosity, a willingness to question and the permission to challenge (and be challenged) is key.

Try, learn, try: new technology, new ways of working, new ways of sharing, new approaches, new techniques, new mindsets. Try, learn, fail, learn. Agility is about always being willing to stretch, and to support others as they find their stretch. Agility requires effort, but the reward is clear. What was the last thing you learnt?

Share: when you succeed, when you fail, as you try. Work out loud. Bring your experience to your communities and make them stronger. Be part of the '*sense-making*' process. Sharing is a differentiating behaviour in the Social Age: share widely, but share wisely. Interpret what you share to be relevant to the audience. Contribute to the signal, not the noise.

Be humble: learning is about humility. You know an answer, but not all the answers. Behave without expectation of reciprocity. Add value to the community, because the community will pay it back when you need it. Invest when you can.

Tell stories: craft your experience into stories that transmit wisdom. Short stories, long stories, stories in the moment or longer and more reflective pieces. Explore co-creation. Writing stories together is a great way to learn. Experiment with stance, tone of voice and genre. Learn from the stories other people share.

Be fair and protect: fairness is about doing what's right, not what a system or set of rules tells you to do. Fairness often sits within an open space. It can be hard to find. Continue to search. Search for inequality and make it right. If you don't know how to make it right, strive. Because the battle for fairness is our own battle, and the duty to protect is yours. Not in a system, not in a process, not in a reporting button. It sits with every individual.

'Understanding Amplification' For Social Businesses, Leaders and Learners

I was never much good at organised games at school. To be honest, I just wasn't very engaged. Whilst the other boys were charging around the rugby pitch in the rain, sliding through the mud and acquiring scars to carry with pride, I was apt to be daydreaming at the back, looking at the trees or pondering why the ball was an odd shape.

'Stoneface' Stoneham, the games master, had one strategy to deal with this: shouting. He was not a subtle man, he was more used to motivation by volume than leadership by consensus, and certainly not a man to stare at trees or ponder the meaning of ellipsoids. Not unless it would help you kick it over the goal line, anyway.

So Stoneface would stand there bellowing at me and I'd stand there in my wet socks with mud up my legs pondering life, whilst we both failed to comprehend each other until it dawned on me that shouting ever more loudly will probably not get you far in life.

And anyway, why shout loudly when all you really need to do is be amplified by others?

Amplification is the secret heart of social: it's what makes memes travel around the world, what makes adverts go viral, it's what gives good ideas a life of their own and ensures that bad ones sink. Amplification is what everyone wants, what everyone needs, but only a few can get.

Except old Stoneface, of course. I think he shouted because he was just unhappy. I'd have been unhappy dealing with my ten-year-old self too.

Understanding amplification is important, because not everyone amplifies your messages. In fact, hardly anyone amplifies, and only a tiny percentage of those who do will be relevant for your particular messages, because amplification is contextual: different people amplify different things. Social Leaders need to understand how their vision is amplified, Social Businesses need to understand the perils of amplification, Social Learners need to identify strong amplifiers and include them in their personal learning networks.

The Social Age is tied up in networks: connected individuals, each of whom, in turn, is connected out to others. It's a tangled web we weave and it's changing every minute of the day.

Building and curating the shape and structure of your network is important, as is your ability to shape and structure your messages to encourage amplification. Because everyone curates the content they share, to a greater or lesser extent, we can start to differentiate between those who add value to everything that passes them by, and those who simply recycle content. We can start to see those who are discerning in their messages and those who simply aren't.

In the democratised age of publishing, everyone can publish, but we have lost the editorial role. Well, to a large extent, this role is picked up by the community, particularly the amplifiers. People who are discerning of what they see, as well as active in amplifying that which they like, act as the first-line editors of social content.

Whenever we (or organisations within the social marketplace) broadcast anything to our communities, some people consume (and leave it at that), whilst others amplify. The amplifiers may be shouting into empty space (if they are not well connected or have a low reputation for amplifying without discernment) or they may be speaking to the converted, preaching to a crowd that is hungry for more.

The great thing about connecting with amplifiers who have a strong reputation is that they have themselves curated a focused community: in theory, you can get a higher hit rate within those focused communities than you can directly to the whole world.

In the Social Age, those people who are more adept at engaging with the amplifiers, and who curate a strong reputation for adding value to what they amplify, will be more influential, have a greater ability to build reputation. Organisations need to understand that this will not happen just through their formal channels, but through the informal ones too: people who sit entirely outside formal hierarchies of power and authority may curate strong reputations and build influence, entirely subverting formal structures. This can scare people significantly.

When messages are amplified within a community, they tend to gain momentum. The greater the amplification, the greater the momentum, especially when every discerning amplifier projects your messaging into ever more refined communities, who may share interests and be more amenable to what you have to say.

Eventually all but the most engaging messages will die out. But you can certainly influence how far your messages get, by crafting them well and curating a strong first-line network, by being an effective amplifier yourself and by engaging with others, by building your own reputation and facilitating others to build theirs.

Getting a good grasp on amplification and momentum, much like getting a good grasp on a slippery, mud-covered rugby ball, will get you far in the game.

Becoming a Social Leader: organisational strategies for engaging and retaining talent

To face the challenges of the Social Age, a time when change is constant and innovation and creativity key for survival, organisations need Social Leadership. Social Leaders will enable them to develop and maintain their agility, their ability to respond to change, to innovate and be creative, to survive. They need people who are fluent in the technology and social conventions that enable the formation of communities and the engagement of those communities with the everyday challenges of the business.

But Social Leaders may not arrive through traditional development channels. They may emerge from within or need to be attracted from outside the business. Social Leaders may not be identified or developed through existing succession planning efforts.

From an organisational perspective, we have to recognise that, as we move ever further away from the concept of *'jobs for life'*, we can no longer expect to have a monopoly on leadership development. People are owning their own careers, outside the formal hierarchies of positional power and authority, which are, in any case, crumbling under the agility and effectiveness of more social models. We need strategies to attract great candidates from outside the organisation, and we need a curriculum to develop Social Leadership internally.

Social Leaders are founded more on their ability to create meaning than on their pure knowledge, something that we need to keep in mind when we go looking for them. Whilst historically the organisation has used formal training as a chance to impart both knowledge and skills, today it's worth thinking more about providing mentoring and challenge.

Knowledge itself is easy to come by, and skills are forged in the fires of practice, the reality of constant change and deadline-driven projects. What are harder to come by are great mentors and appropriate challenge, so by providing these an organisation can become magnetic to talent (both internally, to retain emergent Social Leaders, and externally, to attract them).

In the Social Age we see that people are more attracted to formally recognised qualifications, so simply saying we run an eighteen-month leadership programme for top talent may be less effective than saying we provide internal and external mentors (and support your time to work with them), we provide dedicated spaces for challenge (internally for cohorts and with external expertise bought in for specific units) and we support you to eventually pursue an external qualification (recognising that nobody will be here forever and that transferrable qualifications are meaningful).

Social Leaders can be recognised by having a strong reputation: they will be active in communities and able to use that engagement to be more effective, individually and within teams. It's a trait of Social Leaders that they don't just develop their own skills, they have the humility and foresight to develop others, recognising that teams are stronger than individuals.

The foundations of Social Leadership are supported by a network of mentors, people who help emergent Social Leaders to define the spaces to work in and moderate their actions with the experience of others. Once the foundations are in place, and reputation is building, it's community and knowledge management that are key. Fluidity of role within community is important: because Social Leaders don't rely on positional authority, often they are not in a leadership role at all, and certainly there is no assumption that they will be.

Knowledge management is important because Social Leaders are islands in the sea of dross that flows through official communication channels. They filter and sort, adding value to anything they pass on. Contextualising information and making it relevant to the audience, as well as using data-driven conversations to influence and support.

Authority is not the end point of Social Leadership: it's a by-product of the activities that make a leader. If you are agile, if you are supported by appropriate mentors and engaged within communities (in fluid roles, adding value), if your approach to knowledge management is strong and you contextualise knowledge appropriately, then your authority will grow.

For organisations, the challenge is twofold: firstly, to recognise that the existing, formal hierarchies are changing, that the leadership models of the twentieth-century Knowledge and Manufacturing Ages may not suit the twenty-first-century Social Age, and secondly, to recognise that we don't forge Social Leaders through courses and accreditation, we do it through mentoring, reward and the creation of spaces for talent to thrive.

Whilst the very nature of work is adapting to the realities of life today, whilst we see increasing focus on ethical business and collaborative working, there has never been a better time to assess your stance on Social Leadership.

The Social Business: aligning Social Learning and Leadership to the values-driven organisation

There's a shift towards a more social culture of business: not just engaged in social spaces, but values driven and responsible. Being proud of your credentials is no longer the preserve of niche cosmetics manufacturers and cooperatives: it's now on the mainstream agenda of many global organisations.

Values driven? It's about deeds, not just words. It's about a Social Contract between employer and employee, about recognising that in the Social Age this relationship may be impermanent, but it can persist over time through different iterations. Employed, in the community, or freelance. Organisations no longer exist in splendid isolation, but rather within an ecosystem of associates and a community of brand. Their reputation is forged in this space: by their leaders, their teams, their competition and the wider community of consumers.

So you need to be engaged. As an organisation, you need to be engaged in a responsible way with an authentic tone of voice in the social spaces that surround you. As an individual, you need to curate your reputation (to use the principles of NET) and as a leader you need to facilitate the relationship between the two.

Social Learning and Social Leadership come together to support the values-driven business, because the narrative of the business has to be co-created and co-owned by the teams and communities. In the Social Age, brand is a collaboratively defined experience, not solely owned by the organisation, so only authentic engagement with community will allow the building of a social brand.

Learning needs to be broader and wider than previously thought: it's about engagement over time, about supporting the holistic development of the individual, so not just needs-driven and planned learning, but also learning driven by curiosity or forged within communities.

I believe that the values-driven business, a business that is responsible and engaged, can only be grown by the organisation if it finds and develops a Social Leadership model and enhances its formal learning interventions with Social Learning spaces. It's a Social Model of learning to deliver the Social Business.

Social Leadership: communities and meaning

We don't just belong to one community: in the Social Age, we belong to many. Maybe there was a time when we all lived in caves and gathered around campfires to skin mammoths, when we were constrained by being in just one tribal group, but today our membership is wide and varied. Some are social groupings, based around old university friends, school mates, chess clubs or gardening, whilst others based around our offices at work, some around specific interests (like car mechanics or yoga) and others around individual projects.

Sometimes our interactions with these groups are just for fun, whilst at other times they are focused around problem solving for specific challenges.

We interact within communities to create meaning, in the moment. That's what the Social Age is all about: moving beyond pure knowledge to finding the meaning and taking transformative action.

Social Leaders understand this. They take facts, previous experience and knowledge and

share this, within their communities, to create meaning: they curate and interpret this information and make it specific to the audiences that they share it with. This act of curation and sharing builds their reputation, and reputation subverts more formal models of authority. And if there isn't a community there to do this in, they form one for the duration of the project (they have the Social Capital to form and develop these).

The challenge for organisations is this: they need to identify and cultivate Social Leadership skills, whilst at the same time being magnetic to new talent. They need to create and tolerate the socially collaborative spaces that these communities need, from both a technological and a moderation perspective. They need to be seen as creative and innovative places to work, true Social Age businesses with a mindset and policies to prove it.

Today, agile social workers, innovative Social Leaders, have choices: they can work for you or they can work elsewhere. Where do you want them to turn? Can you afford to lose them?

Not all relationships are equal.

Relationships come in all shapes and sizes: but they are not all equal. We form communities around a wide variety of subjects and needs, some based on shared values, some on reciprocal exchange, some formed around contracts, some on shared hope, but the foundations affect the nature of interactions and ways that those communities respond to change.

Social Leaders need the ability to engage within multiple communities and to form spontaneously emergent ones around specific challenges. Social Learners need to engage effectively within communities to form consensus and develop learning narratives. Communities develop momentum for change and act as first-line support as it unfolds. It's worth us understanding how relationships are formed within them and what their foundations look like so that we are better able to nurture them.

There needs to be an element of trust within relationships, but it's naive to think that this means trust without conditions: look at the type of relationship we have with our banks or insurance companies. We trust them with our money, but only within a framework of regulation. We trust them because there is a mechanism to deal with failures of trust.

Relationships may rely on blind faith, founded upon reputation, or may include shared goals and values. There may be an expectation of reciprocity, but, equally, a relationship may be altruistic or based purely upon monetary reward with no expectation of anything else in return.

Why every business needs Social Leaders

Social Leadership is a style of leadership that fosters innovation and creativity, collaboration and effectiveness. It does this by focusing on nine components that, together, develop the mindset and skills required to build Reputation and Authority in the Social Age. It's founded on a belief that the ecosystem we live in is changing: that our relationship with knowledge has evolved, that your value is no longer founded on what you know, but rather on your ability to create meaning, your ability to function in formal and informal networks to create momentum and support and sustain change. Social Leaders are collaborative and tell powerful stories.

In other words, '*fit for purpose*' no longer means getting trained up and then operating on a level playing field until your next promotion. The agile learner and the agile business both need to develop and rehearse the skills required in a world in constant change.

Why do we need agility? Because process and control will not deliver the space for reflection and experimentation that is needed to be excellent. Agility is about iteration and feedback, it's about co-creation and collaboration. It's about a culture that supports learning from mistakes and that tells stories of its success.

Social Leaders will be both found and grown within the business, but also need to be identified and attracted from outside. A business that supports social ways of working will be magnetic to this type of talent, and when you're magnetic, it makes life much easier!

The formal networks and hierarchies that defined the businesses of the past are being swept away by changing dynamics of power, knowledge and authority. People build reputation within communities, based upon their ability to curate appropriate content, create strong narratives, share these appropriately and support others in the co-creation of meaning from these stories. Businesses need to be able to engage in these semi-formal and informal spaces, whilst still retaining credibility in formal ones. We see time and again instances where businesses believe that this is simply about social media policies and having a Facebook page, but it's far, far beyond that.

When we build a population of engaged leaders who are able to lead in socially collaborative ways, we build the foundations of agility and creativity that will sustain the organisation into the future. Engaged with its employees, leaders and communities.

The Reputation of Social Leaders

Reputation is forged in our communities, founded upon our actions, our choices, our stance. It's about our ability to curate great content, add layers of context and share it effectively, to be known as someone who gets things done, and does that collaboratively and whilst developing others. In the Social Age, reputation forms a bedrock of leadership and isn't hierarchical or bestowed by others. It's earned through actions and deeds.

Many leadership development activities focus on behaviours and skills, but miss the broader picture: leadership is curated. We make active choices what ethical and behavioural stances we will take on any subject. We choose who to bring into our networks and who to exclude, who to develop and who to avoid. Our choices around community building are not accidental, they are considered.

To effectively develop Social Leaders, we need to support them in building their reputation, by teaching the concepts of curation, narration and storytelling.

Our reputation is highly portable: it comes with us wherever we go and into whatever communities we engage with, so it's worth exerting some effort to get it right.

Social Leadership resides with individuals: whilst older forms of positional or subject-based authority were dependent upon longevity, Social Leadership and reputation can bypass all of these.

The challenge for organisations is this: how do you support your leaders in building their reputation? It needs investment in Socially Collaborative Technologies, in training for the core skills of curation and storytelling, and in a mindset that recognises the evolving nature of work.

Organisations that get this right will be truly agile, able to benefit from the creativity and agility that Social Leadership brings.

How Social Leaders fight fires wisely

A busy day today, supporting a team under pressure. I recognise in myself some patterns of behaviour, some of them constructive, others less so. It turns out I'm far from perfect under pressure, but am, at least, in good company.

So today the blog is late, it's evening and I'm sitting in an office, thinking about dinner. I'm hungry, but wanted to share some thoughts on how Social Leaders fight fires.

The premise of Social Leaders is to be agile, to create meaning in the moment and to do it again, differently, tomorrow. So when better to do this than under pressure? Social Leaders work in communities: they collaborate and co-create solutions. They don't rely on hierarchical authority, but instead build consensus in communities and communicate effectively. They recognise patterns, both in themselves and in others, but work to build out of that, providing support and acting with humility.

In the Social Age, we leave nobody alone: we recognise that responsibility is shared and that we are stronger when we acknowledge our weaknesses. Ego has a limited role in a highly functioning team. That doesn't mean we can't build our reputation, but it has to be based on the nine core principles of Social Leadership: we curate our position, we tell effective stories and share them wisely. We operate in communities, build our reputation and develop our authority based upon that. We co-create meaning, build the Social Capital of others (whilst supporting them with humility) and collaborate effectively.

And at the end of the day, the only fires we recognise are the ones we sit around to share our stories, to build our team community and learn together. This is not an ideal notion: if we are wise, we learn to fight fires effectively. Wisdom trumps stubbornness and dogma every time.

Social engagement and exclusion

There's a competitive advantage to being connected: communities form around common interests and needs and the price of membership is always balanced or exceeded by the benefits it brings. In communities, we can produce more, distribute fairly, provide support and care, have strength in numbers and shape the world to suit our needs. Whilst yesterday's communities were anchored in coal mines and sources of minerals, today we have just as many centred on subject matters, common goals and shared needs. Our online communities are many and varied.

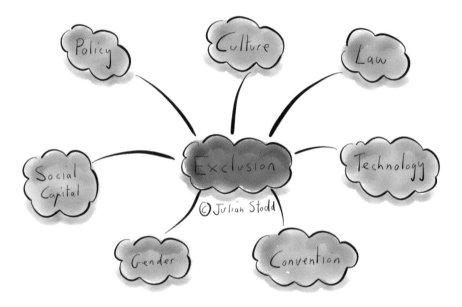

For leaders, social engagement is essential: the premise of Social Leadership is that we create meaning, we build reputation, and hence, authority, through our communities. Whilst this socially moderated power does not always replace formal authorities (although it may fully subvert them), it's certainly important and may be the difference between success and failure in any given role.

For society, social engagement brings benefits and perils. The benefit is that it's easier to rally to a cause, be it fracking or immigration, human rights or The X Factor. The peril? That we may inadvertently create chasms of opportunity between the 'haves' and 'have nots', separated not only by access to technology, but also by lack of Social Capital and even freedoms to participate.

So every action to create and share should be accompanied by an awareness of the hidden society, the disenfranchised and voiceless. Social Leadership includes a responsibility to form communities, to reach out and counter the forces that separate and divide.

Socially engaged leaders and workers are pioneering new approaches to '*working out loud*', sharing their iterative thought processes and the inner workings of their personal narratives. This approach, within a supportive community, is powerful and rewarding, relieving us of the fear of mistakes and supporting us to emulate all or part of a particular journey. But for the disenfranchised, especially those who are powerless through institutional convention or coercion, culture or law (for example, societies where women are forbidden or prevented from contributing), such freedoms are a long way off. The gap between the socially engaged free elements of our global society and the socially repressed or disenfranchised may be growing wider.

Social Collaborative Technology breaks down barriers: geographies no longer divide us, language may not separate us as instantaneous translation comes ever closer, knowledge is no longer hidden away but rather served up to us on smartphones and tablets and parsed into ever more digestible chunks. We no longer need a printing press to make a statement and no longer need a TV station to broadcast it. We are empowered by technology to learn, to form opinions, to craft our stories and share them widely. Or at least we are if we are socially engaged.

In my optimistic moments, I see that this engagement is pervasive and has great momentum: I doubt that even the most oppressive regimes can block access forever, but maybe at a more local level we miss the problems. Within our own organisations, what forces prevent membership? Do we discriminate on grounds of age, of grammar, of department? Do our policies on social media and privacy prevent sharing and the formation of opinions, or encourage it.

Changes in communication technology drive changes in wider society: our ability to form and belong to communities changes how we live and work. These impacts are felt at a micro and macro level. On a personal and local basis, our social relationships are transformed by social networking sites that expand and enhance our ability to maintain a volume of loose social ties, whilst at a macro level our freedoms to challenge authority are enhanced by the ways that ideas permeate and turn viral. Wikileaks would not have happened without a raft of underlying technologies and changes in our relationship with knowledge.

The Social Age is facilitated by technology, but formed on an understanding that engagement will be free and unhindered. Where access is prevented, by convention or law, through coercion or poverty, opportunities are lost and people are left behind.

The humble leader

By enabling others, we succeed. Leading with fairness, kindness and a willingness to give without expectation of reciprocity in the moment is the sign of a strong Social Leader. Finding the meaning, finding the path through the challenges to our balance, acting with honesty and integrity (instead of just putting the words on a poster in the lift) are signs of a true Social Leader. Holding formal authority is just an incidental fact. Social Leaders may have no formal authority, but rather, their power is granted by the community, consensual, in the moment.

The best leader I've met this week was in a cafe in London. He worked with a team of three, taking orders, making coffee, directing the team. He did so with great efficiency, and with laughter. I became aware of this the moment I walked in: he radiated energy. He engaged each customer differently: some by name, some with a question, all with a smile. And he did the same with the team. Gently directing the action without ever giving an order. You might think it's easy to work in a coffee shop: maybe you're right. But it's probably hard to do that whilst earning smiles and jokes from your team.

Smiles and jokes? Incidental to effectiveness, surely? Maybe, but central to culture, I suspect. Culture that is co-created in the moment by everyone within an organisation.

Culture that is both fragile and enduring: fragile in that it's susceptible to pressure when formal authority is stamped upon it, but durable in the relationships that sit underneath it. The bonds that hold individuals together, which may be far stronger than those bonds that hold individuals within the organisation.

Social Authority is consensual, granted by the community, in response to our actions over time. We earn it. And continue to earn it. It cannot be bestowed or bought. But humility? Humility is a willingness to learn, a willingness to be questioned, to collaborate, to support. Humility is not a sign of weakness, but rather a sign of agility and strength, in that you cannot gain trust and Social Authority through volume and direction alone. You can direct people to do a job, to complete a task, but you can't inspire them with orders.

We all have a reputation: what yours is is within your control, if you act with consistency and openness. Striving for what's right, not just what's easy. Sometimes this requires us to navigate a path: between what the organisation mandates and what we know to be true. Organisations can give us a frame to operate within, but it's our actions within that frame that determine whether we are fair, whether we treat people as equals, whether we do what is right.

For example, you can employ someone unfairly. If we know there are gender pay gaps within our business, and we employ a woman at a lower rate, we are consciously endorsing the difference. We can rationalise it any way we like, but failing to address a known wrong is tantamount to committing that wrong ourselves. Sure, we can come up with a host of reasons, but if those reasons leave the end results with the new starter on a lower pay grade, we have failed. We have handed the inequality on to the next tier, rather than resolving it ourselves. And that's not right or fair. Solving the issue is not necessarily required to be fair, but acknowledging it and trying to is. We may have to run with a bad decision, but our willingness to stand up for what is right will determine the light in which others see us. Are you perpetuating inequality, or attempting to subvert it?

The image of the grey-suited leader, stern and often male, is enduring, although not endearing. Testosterone-driven leadership (which usually incites people to try to lead with strength and power) is all well and good, but it's just one aspect of great leadership, and not necessarily the hammer to crack every nut. Social Leadership is not an alternative to formal, but rather supplementary, and it's the style of leadership we use in social spaces, the sense-making spaces that will help us to be more effective.

Social Leaders are facilitating and enabling: they seek to make others successful, through their actions, their words, their generosity of time and spirit and their actions even when nobody is watching. The do so in the belief that action creates culture, so if we are not actively striving to do what is right, we are actively eroding or, at best, leaving static, the existing culture. And who wants to be known for doing nothing when there is so much to improve.

The three levels of Narrative

Across the writing on the Social Age, I talk about levels of narrative – personal, co-created and organisational – so I felt it was time to capture and define them properly. The ways we use stories are many and varied, but this framework is intended to help us plan and execute in a structured and rigorous way. The levels of narrative are complementary: the personal feeds into the co-created and, if we architect it right, the co-created and personal both inform the organisational story.

In the old world, organisations wrote stories and did them to people: in the Social Age, those stories should be co-created and co-owned. The organisation may frame them, may create a narrative space, but the detail, the story itself, should be collaborative. Why? Because everyone should have a voice if we want them to be invested in its success. Because every voice helps us with our sense-making process.

Personal narrative is our story of learning and change over time: it's about both formal and social learning opportunities, about what we take from them, what we do with that, how we execute it, prototype and experiment, rehearse and learn, and how we make our marks in the sand over time. The personal narrative is written by the individual, over time, and forms the first reflective space.

Co-creation is what happens within our communities. It's about curation, storytelling, sharing; it's about challenge and support, critique and cross-linking. Our communities help us carry out this sense making, creating meaning out of the deluge of information and inputs. The co-created group narrative is co-written by everyone in the community: it's shared and iterated rapidly. It reflects the best sense-making effort in that moment, but not the best we will ever do. That's the beauty of co-creation: it evolves as circumstance changes. It's adaptive and dynamic, and that's why, if we unleash the power of co-creation, we can become agile.

The organisational narrative is a meta-narrative: instead of being written at the top and pushed down, it should be an analysis and reporting on the personal and co-created narratives produced by the community itself. This is why I say in the Dynamic Change Framework that organisations have to be brave enough to relinquish control. If you maintain rigid control, you can't truly co-create, and without co-creation, we are just broadcasting, which is a passive format.

I'll break each of these levels out further over time, helping to build an understanding and approach, as well as looking at the dynamics that can interfere with, or amplify the success of, this approach.

The concept will be familiar if you have read my other explorations of the Social Age:

In Social Leadership, we look at co-creation in terms of how a Social Leader forms or engages in various communities, taking a different role in each, and co-creates solutions. We look at how the Leader facilitates each of these voices to be heard, supporting storytelling in each space.

In Social Learning, we look at the co-creative approach to learning, making sense, together, of the formal elements and contextualising them to be relevant to us in our everyday reality. We write personal and co-created narratives to share learning back out into the tacit wisdom of the organisation.

In the Dynamic Change work, I talk about co-creating and co-owning the future state, using stories to break through the resistors to change and writing the future stage, the new organisational narrative, together.

By architecting our work in line with, or taking account of, the three levels of Narrative, we can tie into the ways stories form, are shaped and amplified, ensuring we can gain momentum in our work.

The three levels of Narrative: personal narrative

The importance of finding the space and time to write a personal narrative is that it's our first reflective space, our first opportunity to consider what we have learnt, how we are changing, how we see other people change, what they are doing, what we can do differently, how it works out when we try, what we will take on board and do again next time, and so on. It is, in essence, a stream of consciousness: one that tracks what we feel, do and say and that shapes the stories we share.

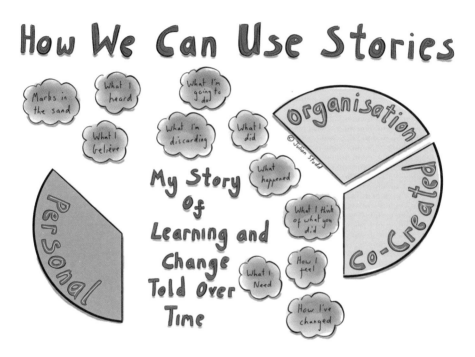

This may sound either self-indulgent or redundant, but it's far from it: our personal narrative is the best way for us to lay out our markers in the sand, to chart our change over time. It's easy to assume that we constantly learn and adapt, but the reality is that many of us are trapped to a large extent by our habitual responses. Writing our personal narrative over time allows us to see these patterns.

In practice, what does this look like? Where there are formal applications of this narrative framework, when we engineer a personal narrative layer into a Scaffolded Social Learning design, as well as informal applications, where we are simply #WorkingOutLoud, sharing our backstage thinking as we go.

You can read about Scaffolded Social Learning over on the blog at www.julianstodd. wordpress.com, but, in essence, it's an approach to learning design that weaves layers of co-creation and discussion around formal '*broadcast*' elements. In the Scaffolded Social Model, we use personal narratives to track an individual's learning over time, we use the co-created narrative to capture the discussions and sense-making activity of the community and, if we are agile, we continuously rewrite the organisational narrative to reflect the conversations within the community.

For example, I recently shared a case study around Scaffolded Social Learning design that looked at how we may work with leaders to understand asymmetric competition. If the organisation is agile, it will read all the narratives that these leaders write together, and it will adapt its own view of competition as a result. In essence, in an agile organisation, the story is co-written by the community, framed by the organisation. In a more lethargic organisation, the story is written by people in the hierarchy who think they know best, then broadcast to the team. That may be a good start, but it's only ever half of the story.

Look at Wikipedia: co-created and co-owned wisdom, the tacit knowledge of the community made visual. In the old world, we wrote the story then published it: in the new world, we publish, then continue to evolve, so what you read today is the most recent version of our unfolding understanding. But it will never be as complete as the story we rewrite tomorrow. That's how most news sites work now: instead of publishing each day, they have moved to publishing a morning and evening edition, then abandoned paper publishing altogether and update constantly. Each story is written and rewritten, and typically, each also includes space for comments, so the community can contribute too. Indeed, the rise of the citizen journalist is one of the defining features of the Social Age.

Within a typical learning programme that is designed according to the Scaffolded Social Learning model, we see the personal layer and the co-created community layer of narrative in place.

We also have the notion of personal narrative in Social Leadership, the style of leadership we need in the Social Age: here, it's something we write over time and share with our community as part of our dedication to #WorkingOutLoud and sharing our learning back to the community. For Social Leaders, the most important aspects to consider are the stance of their narrative, the tone of voice that they take, and the ways they share the stories that they write.

The three layers of narrative also make an appearance when we consider the Dynamic Change Framework: in this work, I describe how an agile organisation will co-create and co-own the future state, drawing on the insight and thinking of their community. Within this framework, the objective is to support everyone in writing their own version of that future state and working together to co-create a shared narrative. So the individual stories contribute to the overall organisational level of the narrative.

The applications I've described above all form part of the *'formal'* application: where we are using the levels of narrative within a framework, to help us achieve an overall goal. But we can also consider how personal narrative can be used outside this, in more social and ongoing ways.

The principles of Working Out Loud are simple: we let people see behind the scenes, not just showing our performance, but sharing the rehearsals. John Stepper has done some superb work around this, creating a simple framework to achieve this. In my language, we use personal narratives as we Work Out Loud (sometimes abbreviated to #WorkingOutLoud or #WOL on Twitter) not only to explain what we did, but also to shape our thinking as we work out what we are going to do. It's not just a documentary, passive storytelling approach, but rather part of our sense-making and thinking process.

For me, the blog is my personal narrative and sense-making space: I write it primarily to give my ideas shape, but also to air them to a wider audience (outside my own head) and see how they land. Sometimes well, sometimes less so, sometimes those thoughts fade without a trace. The ones that survive tend to iterate: we start with an idea, ill formed and embryonic, and share it in our personal narrative: if it's strong enough, if we reflect and nurture it, it evolves and takes shape, over time, under the watchful eye of our community.

Of course, we don't have to #WorkOutLoud to benefit from personal narratives: indeed, there are contexts when we wouldn't want to, and shouldn't encourage others to either.

It's only safe to share a personal narrative when we understand the permission we have (or choose the permission that we want to claim) and when we understand the nature of consequence and how much of it we want to take on.

Personal narrative is the first of the three layers, but is by no means the least important: it's the foundation for the other two. If we have no personal narrative, no format or space to capture it in, it's hard to contribute effectively to the co-created narrative. And without a strong co-created narrative, we can't effectively write the meta-narrative of the organisation. So we need to think about it in two contexts: firstly, how we design personal narrative into learning and, secondly, how we create spaces and permission to reflect, Work Out Loud and share our story as we do so.

The three levels of Narrative: co-created stories

The purpose of the co-created narrative is not to drive consensus: rather, it's a record of difference and dissent. It's a news story written by the community, or by looking into and listening to the community, which reflects what is considered important at this time.

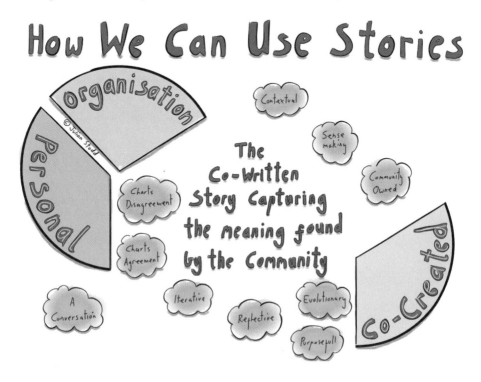

In common with all co-created and community-moderated narratives (such as Wikipedia), it's only valid in the moment: it's not a definitive story that will last forever, but rather, today's version of an evolutionary story. One that will continue to evolve as the different co-creators learn and change. Much as the news is renewed every day, reflecting our current interests and priorities. Co-created stories are not facts: they are interpretations of reality written anew every time. The trick is to realise that organisational stories are not fact either, even if they pass themselves off as such.

There are many ways to capture the co-created narrative of the community: we can ask them to write it, we can ask other communities to write it, we can capture it for them, or facilitate someone else to do so. We can change the stance, the language, the location, the tone of voice and the perspective of the story. These are the tools and approaches at our disposal, each one resulting in a different type of story, a different kind of narrative, but all with one thing in common.

Co-created narratives are owned by the community themselves: in Social Learning terms, the organisation has permission to be in the conversation, but it cannot own the story. This has all sorts of implications: for how we set the conversations up, to where we have them, to what happens with the story once it's written. The rule of thumb is this: if it's a co-created story, you're only half in control. You can frame it, but you can't own it. The benefit? You get to hear the voices you couldn't hear before, speaking with an honest truth. The downside? You might not like everything they say.

I was talking to someone yesterday about a co-creative approach to training customer service: in their model, they have a process for dealing with awkward conversations, and the thrust of the training is to train you in and accredit you on that process. Success is in repetition and mastery.

In an approach using co-created stories, we would still follow the formal approach, but talk about the implementation, share other ideas, prototype and rehearse new behaviours and write our shared story about what to do. And that story may differ between groups. It will still be framed by what the organisation wants, but it will include what the community says. So you end up with variety in behaviours, in thinking and in action, but within a set of parameters that keep it safe, or safe enough.

The person I was speaking to liked the idea, but was worried that people may not ultimately follow the process. And they are dead right: they may not. The trick is to realise that they don't follow it now anyway. Because process never gave excellence, and just because we can't hear what they are doing doesn't mean they are doing what we want. In essence, people are already deviating, we just don't have the benefit of hearing how and why. That's why, under a Social approach, using co-created narrative, we win: we get to hear the stories that go unheard, the wisdom of the community. We may still not like it, but we do at least have a foundation.

We can either rewrite the organisational story to reflect the truth on the ground, or we can work with the group to rehearse, prototype and adopt new behaviours, but crucially, we do it together. So no one side gets to own the whole story.

The three levels of Narrative: the organisational story

The personal narrative is a story of individual change and learning over time. The co-created narrative is the sense-making conversation of the community, shared out to the wider organisation, granting access to this tacit wisdom. The organisational narrative should be a meta-narrative built upon each of the previous two.

In old organisations, the organisational narrative is written at the top and *'done'* to people: it's a traditional model of training, for example, where the organisation creates the syllabus and people complete it, being signed off as *'competent'* when they pass an assessment. Under a co-created model, the organisation has a say in the story, but the true story is co-owned and co-written by the community in partnership with the organisation. The organisational story is then an analysis of all of this.

I often say to people that the biggest challenge to organisations that want to be more *'social'* in their approach is that they need to relinquish control: to step back from owning the story, to be more willing to co-create it. Why? Because it's a fiction that the organisation ever truly knew best: what happened was that people completed formal learning, then went and figured out how to do it in real life, within and alongside their communities. All we are doing under a social approach is getting permission to hear the conversation. It's not that we are giving people a space to be non-compliant: they are already non-compliant, we just have a chance to consider what '*compliant*' means and whether we should evolve it to learn from what people are really doing to solve our problems.

Social Learning is about '*sense making*', it's about how communities take formal knowledge, formal systems, facilitating technologies and then figure out how to make it all work in practice. With the right feedback loops in place, with the right permissions and channels, we get to hear this wisdom, the unheard wisdom that sits within our communities. The communities of people, incidentally, that we employed to do the job in the first place.

So under a Social Model, the organisational narrative is written last, not first, and it reflects the sense-making conversations that we have carried out: it is more about reporting on the truth than aspiring to some unrealistic ideal that never truly comes to be.

In this model, the organisational story, like the personal and co-created stories, is more iterative and evolutionary: this is not one story for all time, but rather interpretation and reinterpretation according to circumstance and situation. Changing stories over time, each one written according to the latest view on the ground.

You'll start to see that this is a very different model of organisational working: less about creating collateral with long shelf lives, more about easy frameworks for updating collateral that reflects the best ideas we have this week. It's co-created in the moment to reflect our current rendition of the truth.

This is how co-created knowledge works: it's like Wikipedia, updated constantly, moderated by the community, relevant in the moment.

Organisations use stories in many ways: to set a vision for the future, to share what is happening and what they want to happen, to show and teach people how to do things, to ask them to do things differently, to communicate with clients and potential clients, as a layer of branding over the whole organisation, to thank people and to attract new people.

All of these stories tend to be formal: all could be made more co-creative, more authentic, more highly valid and more closely linked in to the tacit wisdom of the community.

Social Leaders use stories to take what the organisation wants and make it relevant to individuals, and to take what the community talks about and make it visible to the organisation. It's a two-way street, which is how co-creation works. No one side forces the story.

When undergoing change, organisations use stories to show a vision of the future, but that vision is often abstract, so highly aspirational that I cannot see my place within it. An agile organisation will take a dynamic approach to change: creating spaces and communities where individuals can shape the story and claim their place within it. Instead of fighting for survival, fighting to be part of the change, to own and deliver against it. The organisation needs to tell a different kind of story in this environment: co-written with the team within a framework set by the organisation.

This is not about losing control, it's about finding a shared voice.

The ways that organisations write the organisational story are important: it can be a story told by formal leaders, it can be told by a storyteller, or co-written by the community. It could be in a wiki or blog, or through formal materials. It can be moved around between different people over time. But crucially, it's never nailed to the wall: the organisational story is always co-created and should be a meta-narrative that shows that the organisation is listening to the stories told by communities and individuals at every level.

Story flow

I've outlined the three levels of narrative that we can consider within organisations: personal, co-created and organisational. They are three lenses on the world around us, each from a different perspective and serving a different purpose. Let's consider how they flow, one to the other, each informing and shaping those around it, constantly iterating and evolving as our understanding develops.

These stories are Social Age stories: published then written, not bound in bookends and static on a shelf. They are co-created and dynamic, responsive and changeable. They reflect our understanding today, whilst today keeps changing.

Personal stories are our own stories of learning and change over time: a modern-day diary, recording not wistful Victorian love stories, but rather our reflections, challenges, determination and fear, as we feel it, first hand. It's about setting down a marker today. And today. And today, as each today passes. It's about putting lines in the sand and stakes in the ground: this is what I think is true today, and what I will question tomorrow.

Learning is not something done to us, but rather something we choose to take on: we hear or read or experience new things and go through a cognitive process of filtering, acceptance, rehearsal, testing and adoption. Or rejection. Some things that I believe to be true today I will reject tomorrow. Some things that I know, I am prepared to have proven as true, but are currently in quarantine. Some things I know are not perfect, but they are the best framework that I have, so I continue to use them until a better alternative comes along.

This is how we survive: not in a state of perfect knowing, but through a series of conceptual frameworks and beliefs, wrapped up in a personal schema of how the world works and our place within it. A schema that is remarkably plastic: deformed and reshaped according to experience and need.

So experience, both formal learning and simply engagement in our life, informs our personal story: if we are wise, we find spaces to capture it, to record our thinking over time. We capture the story to see how much it changes.

As we come into our communities, we carry out sense-making conversations, each of which is informed and shaped by our personal narrative. The things we believe to be true, the things we know, the experience we have, all shape the conversation. If we are stubborn, we argue: if we are wise, we debate and construct dialogues that allow us to explore and prototype, rehearse and learn. Then, either through the formal intervention of a storyteller, or through our collaborative storytelling efforts, we capture that co-created narrative. The story of what our community thinks, over time.

This is neither my view nor yours, but rather, it's ours. It's not consensus, but rather debate and dialogue.

Personal narrative informs the co-created group narrative, and, in return, is shaped by the conversation. So in simultaneous birth we create a new personal narrative and a new co-created one, reflecting both sides of our evolved understanding.

This is true learning: not done to us, but done by us. Done with each other.

And, over it all, the organisational narrative: a meta-narrative written out of our personal and co-created group stories. This is the hardest thing for an organisation to achieve: to relinquish enough control to permit us to truly shape the story.

In the old world, learning was crafted by the organisation and done to people: in the Social Age, learning is framed by the organisation, scaffolded, but done within community. Co-created stories that we adopt, adapt or accept, informing our personal story and contributing to the next co-created iteration.

In the old world, we wrote a course and recycled it for five years: in the Social Age, we scaffold a course and co-create the meaning, within that framework, but contextualised by the people enrolled, every time. So the story is refreshed anew every time, iterating its way to relevance and remaining both contemporary and grounded in our everyday reality.

It's a circular path: personal stories inform co-created dialogue. The dialogue informs the organisational story. If a dynamic organisation listens, it creates new opportunity and learning, which, in turn, informs and forms the backdrop to the evolved personal narrative. And around we go.

Crucially, this happens anyway: even if the organisation is not socially enabled and permissive, people still form personal stories and co-create narratives. They just do so to protect themselves from the organisation, which isn't listening, rather than to evolve the organisation. So the only true loser if we restrict or quash nascent social communities is the organisation itself.

In the Social Age, only the agile organisation can hope to survive, can hope to thrive. And to be agile, we need to be able to co-create meaning, to find the story, at every level. And we need to continue to evolve that story to be relevant to us in the moment. A flow of stories that never ends.

The end.

Unheard wisdom

If we just listen in the spaces that we know, we will just hear what we've always heard: is your organisation brave enough to listen to the unheard wisdom?

Often organisations are obsessed with how to control the conversation, to own the story, but the cost of that can be that they never get to hear what's truly being said. Think about the heard voices, voices that come through formal channels: permitted voices of consensus and agreement, often saying what we want to hear or allow them to say. Voices which operate under our control, sanctioned to say what it's safe to hear.

Then think about unheard wisdom: voices with no permission, voices that are silenced through formal repression and moderation. Think about the tacit knowledge within the community that truly knows what it's talking about, and whether we are in the right conversations to hear it. The claimed voices where there is no permission: voices of protest, or conscience. What do we miss if we fail to even listen to them? Voices that may carry great authenticity.

There are so many voices, it's naive to think that only our formal ones have value, command respect. As Social Leaders, we need access to all these conversations, to listen with respect and form our own opinion. Preventing people hearing the story does not make it any less true.

Global perspectives on Social Leadership: fairness

The Social Age is global: take the book. I wrote it in the UK, the Philippines and the US. Mainly in coffee shops. The typographer I found on Twitter. The printer was in Chelmsford, but the actual printing press was in Latvia and it shipped via the Ukraine. The geography was incidental to the relationships and capability that the network provided me.

But whilst the technology connects us, not everything is easily globalised: as we travel, we cross boundaries that are legal, geographical and cultural, some more easily visible than others. Social Leadership is a style that is grounded within communities, but, like all things that touch a community, it requires shared values and purpose, something which may not always exist.

People are different: not just by person, but by location and experience. Working in America is very different from working in London, Singapore or France. Each has its quirks, but none of them are global. Our education systems and social conventions leave us with legacy behaviours and patterns of thinking that are deeply embedded. In some societies, class systems are still strong, whilst in others they are almost entirely devolved. This is not an easy path to tread.

'Right' is not universal: Social Leaders can help drive change, towards fairness

When I was designing the Social Leadership model, I was very conscious of this global perspective and the need to keep it value neutral: I failed. The model is intentionally liberal: grounded in values of equality and fairness. The more I worked on it, the stronger this became apparent to me.

Not all cultures share the same legal frameworks or values of equality as my own. Indeed, even within my own culture, those values are not universally shared, but in the model I present for Social Leadership, they are embodied. Why? Because it's right.

In the news this week, Emma Watson, the Harry Potter actress, has been speaking in an impassioned way about equality for women and how men can be part of this battle. She has had an overwhelmingly positive response from many, but, inevitably, in the semi-secretive and anonymous world of the internet, where technology amplifies our stories, there has been hate and vitriol. This morning, threats to release private photos online. This is bullying, and bullying is wrong.

Much as I love to see our evolved ecosystem of technology as a force for good, I recognise that often it isn't: instead, it is used for control or persecution. Our responsibilities as Social Leaders, let alone as decent citizens, are to fight for right. Which is why I embedded those notions within the Social Leadership model (under '*Social Capital*').

Social Leadership is not a fuzzy or fluffy approach: it's a clear imperative to lead effectively in the Social Age. It's not an alternative to formal, hierarchical leadership styles, but it does recognise that these days those styles deliver a decreased return on investment. The world is changing, and the ways we engage and lead within it need to change too.

Formal hierarchies, relying on formal, positional authority, have limited ability to influence in the social spaces where so much of our lives play out. Social Authority, based upon hard-earned reputation, does have this influence.

At a high level, we can view the imperatives of Social Leadership thus: *care*, *productivity* and *co-creation*. *Care* is about doing the right things and taking people on the journey with us. *Productivity* is about being highly effective. *Co-creation* is about understanding how communities work and our role within them. The full Social Leadership model and curriculum explore these areas in great detail, but for this conversation, exploring global perspectives of Social Leadership, let's stick at the high level.

Whilst legislative frameworks and cultural norms may not be universal, certain principles are, such as trust and its role in bonding communities together. Whilst we may differ in certain aspects, the '*care*' role of Social Leaders is to ensure that nobody is left behind, disenfranchised by technology, status, gender or sexuality. Is this a Western, liberal view? Yes, I recognise that is it, but equally the need for '*care*' isn't, so at least we can identify the space to work in.

Take homosexuality: it's illegal in a lot of countries. Tunisia for starters. Morocco. Egypt. The Seychelles. Barbados (although not enforced). It's a long list. I could go on. Probably until around eighty countries were listed.

Now take the realities of the Social Age: organisations work globally, with offices and tens or hundreds of thousands of employees around the world. So do they treat them equally?

Clearly not: lower pay, worse working conditions, in the worst cases, sweat shops and diminished safety procedures. But it's increasingly hard to get away with it. To trade in the Social Age means social responsibility. You can't hide your cheap labour so easily anymore. Look at Apple, announcing the names of suppliers it suspects are using unethically sourced materials: their reputation takes precedence over their contracts. They recognise the importance of authenticity and social responsibility. But they're also under pressure for working conditions and suicides in the factories that make the shiny products, distanced by oceans from many of those who use them.

The amplification effects of Social mean that these stories spread fast.

So here's the crux of it: in a global business, we will be connected into communities that cross these boundaries. We will work alongside people who have different frameworks of what is right and wrong, or who work under different legal systems.

Is it feasible to work on a team that does this? Or is it a liberal illusion perpetrated by Western organisations operating globally. Can you really have a team functioning where one team member, joining the community from the UK, would be jailed if they were sitting in the same office as someone else on the call from Africa? A pragmatic view would be to ignore the problem and just get on with the work, but that approach lacks integrity.

Social Leaders require high Social Capital, and the Socially Responsible Business should do things that are right, not just things that are required by law.

But what's to say that my version of '*right*' is better than yours. Or someone in Nigeria? I guess we all have our perspectives, and laws that are founded upon them, but some things are clear.

The Social Age is seeing the globalisation of communication and the easy amplification of messages. Change is afoot and it's faster than ever. Organisations need to be productive – that much is universal. They also need to take care of people, because Social Leadership relies on communities and you can't form a community without shared values and intent.

The real challenge for countries is that they will become irrelevant: the nation state, bounded by geography, swept aside in favour of the corporate state or, indeed, the Facebook state. It's not as idle an idea as you may think: Coca-Cola already swept aside the Berlin Wall with promises of pizza and MTV. Consumers tend towards liberalism when it brings with it widescreen TV and smartphones.

It's a matter of respect, really: we each have a right to our beliefs, but there must equally be a responsibility for fairness that underpins them, and we may have to fight for that fairness to be recognised. Which is where '*Social Capital*' in Social Leadership comes in. In the Social Age, in a global business, we can't afford to ignore equality, and need to recognise that our very taking a stance is likely to drive change. Just as Emma Watson chose her stance, surely recognising that there would be a short-term cost (but a huge rise in Social Authority: I've been bombarded with people sharing her video with me).

Social Authority can fully subvert the formal: look no further than the role of Twitter in the Arab Spring. Messages that gain support are loud: the technology facilitates this, but it's the underlying social processes that are significant. If communities really are forged upon shared values and common goals, then social technology puts ownership of these firmly back into the community's hands.

I recognise it's a fine line: I have to declare my liberal position to maintain my own authenticity, but I do believe the Social Leadership model provides a framework for organisations to tackle some of these cross-cultural challenges, with both humility and pragmatism.

It's unthinkable that any liberal Western organisation would allow restrictive views to shape how they treated women or people in same-sex relationships in their head office in London or New York, although it's equally unthinkable that some organisations are willing to benefit from poor labour practices in parts of the world whose voice isn't heard so loudly. These are two sides of the same coin.

Developing Social Leaders, throughout our organisation and around the world, united by shared values of fairness and humility, will help us bridge these gaps. And be more effective as an organisation. It just starts with some simple shared values: of care, to seek productivity and to understand how we work in communities.

Complex issues require diplomatic solutions, but these issues are live in every global organisation today, they're just largely ignored or hidden. Bringing them to the front and living our values will help drive the change to a more equal, Socially Responsible, global society.

Ten things a Social Leader does

Social Leadership is contextual and consensual: it's a type of authority granted by the community, founded upon our reputation and Social Capital. Social Leadership complements formal leadership, but works in places where formal leadership cannot reach: our communities. And that's important because, in the Social Age, it's our communities that will help us thrive.

So what do great Social Leaders do? Here are ten things, for starters:

1. They act from a foundation of humility and kindness, because they recognise that leadership is about helping others to be equal, to thrive, to succeed.

2. They tell compelling stories, because they understand that magnetic stories travel far, whilst formal ones get stuck in the system.

3. They are authentic in their words and actions, no matter who is watching, because they recognise that authenticity is earned, not awarded or bought.

4. They often set aside their mantle of leadership to instead learn, or support others.

5. They fight for what's right, not for themselves, but for their communities.

6. They curate a space: choosing where they will stand and then doing everything they can to make that space theirs.

7. They help frame the new Social Contract, helping the organisation to wield authority through consensus, not weight.

8. They #WorkOutLoud as they go.

9. They reward others graciously, in both formal and social spaces.

10. They measure the change, because they recognise that if they don't measure it, it may not be happening.

Social Leadership is not something soft, something *'nice to have'*, something of an add-on to formal power: it's central to the authority we need to wield in the Social Age to truly lead. Through the permission of our communities.

Aspects of Social Leadership: community

I've spent the day in a workshop with a very dynamic group, exploring how we create the conditions for success around Social Learning communities. As I relax with a cup of tea, watching the sun set over the Dublin skyline, I'm reflecting on what I've learnt.

In the Social Age, we inhabit a range of communities, from the fully formal, defined by the organisation, to the fully social, created by us and invisible to any formal authority. In between are myriad spaces, each serving different purposes, each governed by different rules (some that we own, some that are imposed), each creating different types of story and sharing them in different spaces.

The role of the Social Leader is to help others to succeed: through humility, kindness, a drive for equality and fairness, to facilitate, to empower and enable, to share, to create and grant permission, to nurture and support.

If that sounds like a list of aspirations, then we need to do more: in the old world, we governed with raw power. In the new world, we govern through consensus and permission, recognising that if that permission is not granted, it will be claimed.

Many organisations are inherently unfit for the Social Age: they are well intentioned, but ultimately a product of a bygone age. They are mechanisms of control in a world that does not respect that model of authority. The challenge they face: to become facilitating in every aspect of what they do. To enable people to succeed.

Social Leadership is a multi-dimensional model. At times, the role of a leader is to bring new knowledge to a community, to enlighten and surprise. At times, it's to support, to help others to develop high Social Capital and capability. At times, the role of the leader is to learn. Or to give generously. To share.

Social Leadership is founded upon respect, a respect that is earned, not assumed, because no organisation can bestow respect. It's about the offer to help others succeed with no expectation of reciprocity in the moment. It's leadership that is invested in the community, recognising that, over time, we will reap the benefits of being surrounded by and supported by our community.

Today, the group tended to fall into the processes and mechanisms that would drive success: understandable, but it's important to recognise that the things we think hard about to generate the success may well be the things that block it.

The organisation, the formal leadership, can create the conditions for success, but cannot bestow success. Any true social community needs to co-own and co-create its space, its permissions, its rules. Why? Because Social Learning is about the semi-formal, community-moderated learning that surrounds the formal. So if we seek to maintain too much control, if we try to shape the story too far, it simply becomes a formal story and we drive out the very thing that we seek to experience.

The skills we needed yesterday may still be relevant, but are supplemented by a whole new capability.

In the Social Age, knowledge itself has change, away from the Age of Concentration, when we held it in books and knowledge-management systems, towards a time when it's co-created, dynamic, adaptive and evolutionary, held in wikis, in communities, and accessed, usually through technology, at the moment we need it.

An organisation simply cannot hope to maintain a grasp on all the knowledge it needs to thrive: so stop trying. Abandon control, embrace facilitation. Form, guide and nurture the communities that will take us towards agility. Create the conditions for success: that, surely, is the primary role of a Social Leader.

The new utility: a story about brand in the Social Age

Agility can be about perspective, about being brave enough to climb up high and get a better view. Being brave enough to shout from your viewpoint that the world has changed. Being brave enough to lead an organisation and community through that change. Because, in the Social Age, everything has changed, but many organisations have failed to notice, and those that remain in the dark for too long will be swept aside.

We've seen the emergence of value-led brands, brands that make stuff, for sure, but which are represented by more than simple transaction: they are represented by something more. By community, by stories, by membership and ownership, by an emotional sense of connection. A sense of connection you probably don't feel with your bank or healthcare provider.

Younger, more agile, more innovative organisations, ones that truly grasp the scale of change, recognise that the value they have with their consumers is more a matter of negotiation than broadcast.

Just providing a product or service is no longer enough: instead, we need to add the new utility. Community, relevance, authenticity and responsiveness. On our terms, as consumers.

In the Social Age, the value of a brand is co-created with the community and, largely, the value is held by the community. It's no longer broadcast and owned by the organisation. It's no longer about pushing a brand onto people, but instead it's about adding value to people in meaningful ways.

As technology hauled us into the Social Age, organisations were wont to think that their salvation lay in technology: they invested in infrastructure and hardware, systems that let them sell, that let them deliver, that let them trade. Which was all well and good, but the challenge with infrastructure is that it dates, and, when push comes to shove, it only adds one type of value: transactional.

Infrastructure may get the goods out on time, may provide the service, but it doesn't provide the loyalty or love. That comes through the stories, through the meaning that the organisation provides to the individual.

Take Graze, a UK-based supplier of snacks. Each week, if you are a subscriber, you get a box through the post. Inside it are separate, carefully packaged and playfully named packets of snacks. Nut mixes, dried fruit, flapjacks. It's not utilitarian: it's experience. It's choreographed. You can buy mixed nuts more cheaply and in greater quantities at the supermarket, but you can't get the experience or utility at the supermarket. At Christmas, they didn't send a leaflet trying to sell a credit card: they included a pop-up Santa Claus and snowman. If the nature of the relationship is transactional, you can transact. If it's relationship, what you have to do is nurture the relationship.

Look at what Metro Bank are doing, also in the UK. They deliberately position themselves as counter to normal banking culture: they open their branches late and at weekends, expressing incredulity that other banks don't do the same. They are open about their desire to change the market, indeed, they even have a book about it. Sure, they're a business: they're an evil bank trying to make money, but they are doing it in relationship terms, and at least demonstrating a clear desire to engage in a more relationship-based way. Will they succeed? I suspect it comes down to how they engage over time: if the experience feels fundamentally different over time, then yes. If it feels fundamentally like all the other banks over time, then no.

Take my own bank: when I was in America, I accidentally went into my overdraft and they charged me a fee. When I discussed it with them, I said that maybe they could have phoned me, texted me or emailed me about it. Not just fined me and waited for me to discover it by chance. As I pointed out, when they want to sell me something, they are more than happy to craft an email, post me a leaflet or phone me up. So why not do that when something goes wrong? Transactional is fine, but I don't love them for it.

By contrast, last Christmas I had a flat tyre and went to a chain garage to have it fixed. The guy quickly resolved the problem, but wouldn't take any money for it. He explained that it was just a small thing, a faulty valve, and not worth charging for. I'd have been happy to pay, but instead, he was investing in a different output: a relationship. I always recommend them and go back there now.

This isn't about being just nice, though: it's about how we compete and win in the Social Age. It's about the mindset of your organisation and how agile it is. Broadcast modes of communication, transactional methods of engagement – these are all fine if you want to retain control. They are low risk, in terms of message drift, but high risk in terms of agility.

If you accept that the value of your brand is held within the community, then you need to engage with your communities, both internally and externally, with authenticity and humility.

When eCommerce rolled out, the conversation was about how to get online and sell. Now that the space is established, the conversation has moved on, but many organisations are still focused on their platform, instead of being focused on the utility and brand. Successful organisations are crafting a community based on true value: they are agile with the technology, pragmatic about systems, but highly engaged in brand.

At the heart of the message is this: brand is no longer owned by the organisation. It's substantially owned by the community. Organisations that engage with their community in authentic ways are more likely to forge a relationship based on the new utility: not just transactions, but relationship based and persistent over time.

And agile organisations will understand this: they will see that viewing change as a process will only lead down dead ends. Viewing it as a lifestyle will yield rewards. Agile in technology, agile in mindset, engaged in community and willing to listen.

Postscript

Postscript: Be The Change

Old models of leadership are based within a failing hierarchy: Social Leaders represent a fairer, more equal, more balanced approach. Their authority is wielded with empathy and care, not brute force.

It is our duty to make our world better: to fight for those with no voice, to represent those who are disadvantaged, to strike out where we see persecution, bigotry and bias. It is wrong that organisations treat people like commodities and with contempt, even if they smile whilst doing it.

The Social Age is unforgiving of this: adapt, and be welcomed. Persist with old approaches, retain old models of leadership beyond their sell by date, exploit people for profit, and be damned.

This book is about Social Leadership: a style fit for the Social Age. This is a movement, a change, a new reality. Be that change. Make the world a better place. Start with yourself.

About Julian

I'm a writer, a cartographer of the Social Age. Writing is my way of making sense of things and I write every day, at the blog www.julianstodd.wordpress.com

My work tends to lie at the intersection of formal and social systems: from Social Learning to Social Leadership, Equality and Fairness, Creativity and Innovation, Social Technology, Social Justice and Dynamic Change. I am a generalist, which is a happy space for an explorer to inhabit.

I work with global organisations who are interested in something new. I help them find a way.

I am founder and Captain of the Sea Salt Learning group of companies: helping organisations get fit for the Social Age, through consultancy, products and services.

The Social Age is a movement: a new reality, and this is the time to adapt.

You can find Sea Salt Learning at www.SeaSaltLearning.com

My previous books include:

> *Exploring the World of Social Learning*
> *Mindset for Mobile Learning – A journey through theory and practice*
> *Amsterdam Diary – An exploration of learning culture*
> *Learning, Knowledge and Meaning – The Singapore Diary*
> *Julian Stodd's Learning Methodology – Designing effective eLearning*
> *Music and Learning – The co-creation of meaning*

I present widely at workshops, conferences and webinars. You can find me easily online or follow me on Twitter for details @julianstodd

Social Leadership:
my 1st 100 days

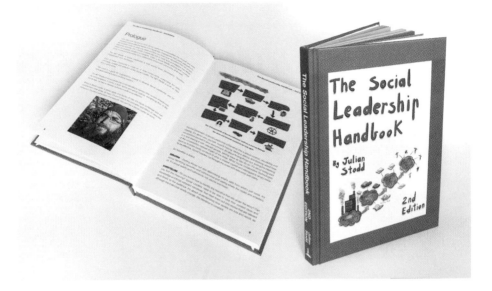

I've had a great deal of interest around the world in how we put the principles of Social Leadership into practice. With this in mind, in 2017, I decided to create a workbook, a guided journey into Social Leadership.

'My 1st 100 days' is a practical guide to developing Social Leadership, for individuals, and within teams. It's structured as a 100 day journey, with each day including some information, a provocation, some questions, and actions to take, much of it out in the real world, making a real difference in your own community.

It's structured around the nine components of the NET model that you've read about in this Handbook: the first ten days explore the 'Foundations of the Social Age', before spending ten days on each of the nine components outlined in this book.

Every tenth day is 'An Action Day', where you are encouraged to put the book down, and put your learning into action.

In this section, I've shared a few days from the '100 days' book. I hope you enjoy it!

Day 1: Are you content?

Look at the organisation around you, the organisation that you work for.

» Are you content with what you see?
» Is it fair? Is it equal? Is it innovative and successful?
» Is it ready to face tomorrow?
» Is it adapted to the realities of the Social Age?
» If you could change one thing, what would it be?

I would change: _____

_____

_____

_____

Ask these questions of someone else: do you have the same answers, or different ones? Across the organisation, would your answers be the same or different? Where is the space to have these conversations? Where is your space to drive change?

Day 2: Power

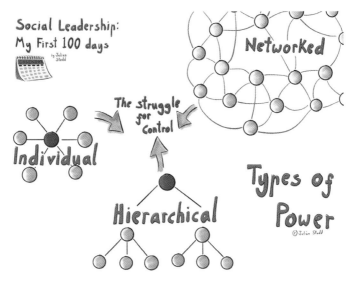

Think about the thing you wanted to change: what power do you have to change that?

There are three types of power: 'Individual' power, which we exert with people we know, 'Hierarchical' (formal) power, which is the type of power the organisation gives us, and 'Networked' power, which is where Social Leadership lives – power and amplification granted to us by the community.

To be the leader you need to be, which types of power do you have, and which do you need to build or earn?

My formal power lives in these places: _____

_____

_____

My networked power lives in these places: _____

_____

_____

Consider which of these you can grow. To gain more formal power, you need a promotion! To gain more Social Authority, you just need to earn it.

Day 3: If not you, then who?

Social Leadership is about taking action, about creating organisations and a wider society that are better: fairer, kinder, more equal, more effective, more inclusive. It's not a dream of a better world: it's the concrete steps to build it.

» Where do you see inequality?
» Where do you see unfairness?
» Where do you see a challenge, either in your organisation, or in wider society?
» Who will solve it?

Does the power to effect change lie just in formal authority, or is some of it about our ability to inspire a community to action. What is the primary type of power you wield in the world?

My formal power: _____

_____

My social power: _____

_____

Day 4: Where is the knowledge?

In the Social Age, knowledge itself is distributed, co-created, dynamic and adaptive. Where does knowledge live in your organisation?

» Where do you go to find things out?

The knowledge lives in this formal place: _____

_____

And in this social place: _____

_____

Think about which of these spaces are formal, held in '*guides*' and '*intranets*', and which are social and co-created, held in people's heads or in communities.

How did you first find out where the knowledge was: through an induction programme, or through the community around you?

Social Leaders are powerful because they are connected to the tacit, tribal forms of knowledge, the lived experience, that flow through the organisation.

Day 5: Generosity

Social Leaders help others to succeed: who can you help today, and how?

I can do this: _____

_____

_____

_____

Our Social Authority is awarded to us by the community: it's not transactional, but rather based upon the reputation that we earn.

The investment we make into our community, through our generosity, is not made in expectation of immediate reciprocity, but rather to help the community grow.